| 汉英对照 |

文明理念篇

Chinese Philosophy

Origins and Contemporary Relevance

中国关键词

KEYWORDS TO UNDERSTAND CHINA

权 威 解 读 当 代 中 国

中国外文出版发行事业局（CICG）
当代中国与世界研究院（ACCWS）
中国翻译研究院（CATL）

新世界出版社
NEW WORLD PRESS

First Edition 2023

Compiled by
China International Communications Group
Academy of Contemporary China and World Studies
China Academy of Translation

Translated by
Han Qingyue

English text edited by
David W. Ferguson and Xu Mingqiang

Cover designed by
He Yuting

ISBN 978-7-5104-7535-1

Published by
NEW WORLD PRESS
24 Baiwanzhuang Street, Beijing 100037, China

Distributed by
NEW WORLD PRESS
24 Baiwanzhuang Street, Beijing 100037, China
Tel: 86-10-68995968
Fax: 86-10-68998705
Website: www.nwp.com.cn
E-mail: nwpcd@sina.com

Printed in the People's Republic of China

《中国关键词：文明理念篇》
编委会名单

Keywords to Understand China:
Chinese Philosophy
Origins and Contemporary Relevance

前 言

中国拥有百万年人类史、一万年文化史、五千多年文明史。在漫长的历史进程中，中华民族以自强不息的决心和意志，筚路蓝缕，跋山涉水，走过了不同于世界其他文明体的发展历程，创造了璀璨夺目的中华文明，为人类文明进步事业作出重大贡献。中华文明源远流长、博大精深，是中华民族独特的精神标识，是当代中国文化的根基，是维系全世界华人的精神纽带，也是中国文化创新的宝藏。中共十八大以来，习近平同志在一系列重要讲话、文章、访谈中旁征博引，运用古代典籍、经典名句阐释中国思想，传递中国声音，在传承和创新中不断激活中华文明经典，赋予其当代价值与意义。

为讲好中华文明故事，增进外国受众对人类文明新形态的了解，"中国关键词多语对外传播平台"组织策划了《中国关键词：文明理念篇》。本篇按照"文明理念从何而来、如何为当代中国所用"的编写逻辑，综合借鉴"中华思想文化术语传播工程"有关成果，择重从修为、民本、善治、交往4个部分，选取80个关键词进行简明扼要的介绍和解读，阐发中华文明讲仁爱、重民本、守诚信、崇正义、尚和合、求大同的精神特质和发展形态，展现中国人"用典一治世"的文化自信，促进中外文明交流互鉴。本书为中外对照版，由于能力及时间所限，在中文词条遴选编写时，难免挂一漏万。为使译文更符合目标语读者的阅读习惯，我们对翻译表达进行了创新探索，旨在提升读者的阅读体验。

“中国关键词多语对外传播平台”是中国外文出版发行事业局、当代中国与世界研究院和中国翻译研究院联合实施的国家对外话语创新重点项目，主要围绕习近平新时代中国特色社会主义思想，进行中文词条专题编写、解读以及多语种编译，通过平面、网络和移动社交平台等多媒体、多渠道、多形态及时持续对外发布，旨在以外国受众易于阅读和理解的方式，阐释中国思想和中国道路，解读中国理念和中国方案。

讲故事需要关键词，讲好中国故事需要中国关键词。让我们用“中国关键词”点击中国、沟通世界。

Introduction

Human activity began in China more than one million years ago. A recognizable culture was in place at least 10,000 years ago and the Chinese civilization dates back more than 5,000 years. Over such a long course of history, the Chinese nation has responded to hardships with self-reliance and perseverance and has followed a path of development distinct from that of other civilizations. It has created a splendid civilization that has made significant contributions to human progress.

China's extensive and profound civilization manifests the cultural identity of the nation. It is the foundation of contemporary Chinese culture, the cultural bond to which all Chinese throughout the world adhere and the treasure that inspires China's cultural innovation.

Since the 18th National Congress of the Communist Party of China in 2012, Xi Jinping has quoted ancient classics, well-known maxims and popular sayings in his speeches, articles and interviews to explain Chinese thought and convey China's voice. The application of classical Chinese philosophy has endowed it with rich contemporary value.

This booklet, *Keywords to Understand China: Chinese Philosophy – Origins and Contemporary Relevance*, has been compiled to tell stories about the Chinese civilization and help global audience better understand its development under socialism. It provides information about the origins and contemporary relevance of Chinese philosophy, with some reference to the outcomes of the Key Concepts in Chinese Thought and Culture Translation and Communication Project.

This booklet has selected 80 keyword entries covering "self-cultivation," "people-centered philosophy," "good governance," and "relations with other nations" to present China's philosophy of benevolence, people-orientation, honesty, justice, concordance, and universal harmony, and the classical allusions behind contemporary governance.

Due to the scope of the work and its tight schedule, there may be oversights and inaccuracies in our selection of entries. To make the English version accessible to an international audience, the English editors have made alterations where they thought it necessary, which could lead to inconsistencies between the Chinese and English texts. Comments and suggestions are welcome for future revisions.

The "China Keywords" platform offers an authoritative guide to understanding contemporary China, and a window into China's political thinking, policies and approach to development, including Xi Jinping Thought on Socialism with Chinese Characteristics for a New Era.

A major national project implemented by the China International Communications Group, the Academy of Contemporary China and World Studies, and the China Academy of Translation, the multilingual platform can be accessed online and on mobile social media platforms.

Keywords are at the heart of any story. "China Keywords" are at the heart of the story of China. We hope that the project will become part of the understanding between China and the rest of the world.

Contents
目　录

修为篇
Self-Cultivation

民本篇

People-Centered Philosophy

善治篇

Good Governance

修为篇

Self-Cultivation

修身、齐家、治国、平天下

“修身、齐家、治国、平天下”，出自《大学》，意指以个人自身修养为基础，先治理好家庭，进而实行仁政德治，治理好国家，更进而安抚和治理天下百姓，最终求得天下太平。在这一层层扩展的过程中，个人的德行和修养与不同层面的政治抱负息息相关。这是中国古代儒家哲学和政治抱负的重要命题，是对“大学之道”的概括，体现了儒家思想由个人到家庭再到邦国进而到天下的逐步递进的道德政治观。

中共十八大以来，习近平多次在讲话中谈及中国知识分子“修身、齐家、治国、平天下”的家国情怀。2014年5月，习近平在北京大学和师生座谈时便引用了这一经典理念，论述如何成就崇高德行和人格，怎样成为经国济世的人才。

Self-cultivation, family management, state governance, and bringing peace to all under heaven

This is a quotation from *Da Xue* (*The Great Learning*). It means that one should first cultivate oneself, then manage the family, govern the state, and bring peace to all under heaven. During this expanding process, a person's virtue and attainment are closely related with their political goals at different levels. This is an important subject of Confucian philosophy and a political ideal of ancient Chinese scholars. The quotation is a good summary of the process of learning and reflects the Confucian view on virtue and politics, starting with an individual and then expanding to the family, the region and the whole country.

Xi Jinping has more than once used this quotation to describe the deep love of Chinese scholars for the country. On one occasion in May 2014, when talking with the faculty and students of Peking University, he referred to this classic concept and encouraged the students to cultivate morality and virtue and prepare themselves for state governance.

格物致知

“格物致知”出自《大学》，是中国传统文化中的重要概念，表达一种对问题穷追不舍的精神，与诚意、正心、修身、齐家、治国、平天下并称“八条目”。基本含义为用自己学得的知识来分析和判断周围的人物和事物，建立完善的三观。引申为懂得“本心”分辨是非真假，并在与周围的人和事接触时更进一步了解自己，更好地找到自己的定位。

2014年5月，习近平在北京大学和师生座谈时谈到，“中国古代历来讲格物致知、诚意正心、修身齐家、治国平天下”，阐发了中国人讲求探究事物原理，从中获得智慧，其目的就是追求诚意、正心、修身、齐家、治国、平天下的境界。

Studying the nature of things to acquire knowledge

This is a quotation from *The Great Learning*. It is an important concept in traditional Chinese culture, meaning that one should conduct a full investigation of a certain issue to get a complete understanding. "Studying the nature of things, acquiring knowledge, making one's purpose sincere, adjusting one's thoughts, cultivating oneself, managing the family, governing the state, and bringing peace to all under heaven," these are collectively known as the "eight essential principles" of ancient Chinese political philosophy.

This quotation indicates that one needs to use knowledge already acquired to analyze and judge the surrounding people and objects in order to build a clear outlook on the world, life and values. The extended meaning is that one should learn to tell right and wrong and discern truth from falsehood, get to know oneself through interaction with other people and surrounding objects, and find one's own position in society.

At the seminar in Peking University in May 2014, Xi Jinping pointed out: Since ancient times, the Chinese people have developed our country through studying the nature of things to acquire knowledge, correcting thoughts with sincerity, cultivating the moral self, managing the family, governing the state, and bringing peace to all under heaven.

知行合一

知行合一，意指认识事物的道理与实行其事是密不可分的。知是指内心的觉知，对事物的认识；行是指人的实际行动。知与行的合一，既不是以知来合并行，认为知便是行，也不是以行来合并知，认为行便是知，而是内有良知则外有良行，知是基础、是前提，行是重点、是关键。知行合一是中国古代哲学中认识论和实践论的命题，主张人的外在行为是受内在意识支配，认为只有由衷向善做到"知"的人，才有外在自发的善"行"。

中共十八大以来，习近平多次强调"知行合一"，要求党员干部既要加强理论学习，走在前列；又要结合实践，干在实处。2019年3月，习近平在中央党校（国家行政学院）中青年干部培训班发表重要讲话时指出，广大干部特别是年轻干部要在常学常新中加强理论修养，在真学真信中坚定理想信念，在学思践悟中牢记初心使命，在细照笃行中不断修炼自我，在知行合一中主动担当作为。

Unity of knowing and doing

This phrase implies the close relationship between what one knows and what one does. "Knowing" refers to one's perception of the objects, and "doing" refers to one's actual deeds.

The unity of knowing and doing does not mean that knowing is doing and knowing can replace doing, or vice versa. It actually means that one should understand things correctly and act accordingly. Knowing is the premise, while doing is putting knowledge to work. The relationship between the two is an ancient Chinese philosophical topic. It is believed that one's conduct is controlled by one's conscience, and one will act properly on one's own initiative only if the true purpose is to do good.

Xi Jinping has emphasized the unity of knowing and doing on a number of occasions. He demands that officials and members of the Communist Party of China (CPC) lead others in theoretical study and apply their knowledge in concrete actions.

Addressing a training program for young officials at the Central Party School (National Academy of Governance), opened in March 2019, he said: Party officials, especially younger ones like you, should have a thorough understanding and good command of theories and strengthen your ideals and convictions through study. You should remain true to the Party's original aspiration and founding mission as Party members, improve yourselves through self-reflection, and take responsibility while applying what you have learned in your work.

仁者爱人

“仁者爱人”的典故，出自《孟子》。“仁者爱人”主要谈论君子与普通人的分别，在于君子能够保持心中的善端，而保持善端的关键，就是将“仁”和“礼”永存心中。“仁者爱人”这句话虽然出自《孟子》，但这一观念却是直接继承孔子的。“仁者”即有仁德的人，是有大智大勇、德行完满、关爱他人、有人格魅力的人。“仁”是儒家文化中最高的道德范畴和境界，其以“爱人”为基本规定，意指“仁”从孝父母、敬兄长开始，进而关爱家族其他成员，并扩大至关心全天下的人。

“仁者爱人”，是2014年5月习近平在北京大学师生座谈会上发表讲话时引用的一句名言。在孟子提炼的思想命题下，其被应用于治国理政，强调君子由亲爱亲人而仁爱百姓，由仁爱百姓而爱惜万物。

The benevolent man loves others.

This allusion comes from *Meng Zi* (*The Book of Mencius*). The Confucian thinker, statesman and educator Mencius (c. 372-289 BC), also known as Meng Ke, talked in the book about the difference between a man of virtue and an ordinary person: The man of virtue always treats others with kindness, because he has *ren* (benevolence) and *li* (rites) in his heart.

This is a well-known saying attributed to Mencius, but the idea originally came from Confucius (551-479 BC), also known as Kong Qiu, a thinker, educator and statesman and the founder of Confucianism. The benevolent man has virtue, wisdom, courage, integrity and personal charms, and cares for others. *Ren*, or benevolence, is the highest moral value and greatest virtue cherished in Confucian culture. Its basic meaning is to love others. One should show filial piety to one's parents, respect one's elder brothers, and extend love and care to other family members and eventually to everyone else under heaven.

This is one of the quotations from Chinese classics cited by Xi Jinping at the teacher-student seminar in Peking University in May 2014. Since ancient times, this shrewd observation has been applied in state governance, reminding the rulers to love the people as they love their own families and to extend such love to all beings under heaven.

上善若水

“上善若水”语出《道德经》，意指至高的善德善举就如同水的品性，默默滋养世间万物而不争强斗胜。老子以水的柔弱之性比喻至善的执政者应有的品德。执政者面对百姓，应该像水之于万物，辅助、成就百姓而不与其相争，后多指为人处世时能像水一样滋润万物，尽己所能帮助他人却从不争名逐利，或者具有坚忍负重、谦卑居下的品格。

2014年11月，习近平在亚太经合组织领导人非正式会议欢迎宴会上指出，2000多年前，老子说“上善若水，水利万物而不争”，意思就是说最高境界的善行就像水一样涓涓细流，泽被万物。亚太经合组织以太平洋之水结缘，我们有责任使太平洋成为太平之洋，友谊之洋，合作之洋，见证亚太地区和平、发展、繁荣、进步。

Great virtue is like water.

This comes from *Dao De Jing* (*Classic of the Way and Virtue*), also known as *Lao Zi* (*The Book of Lao Zi*). It means that the greatest virtue is like water, nourishing all things without competing with them.

Lao Zi (dates unknown), or Li Er, a thinker of the Spring and Autumn Period (770-476 BC) and the founder of philosophical Daoism, used this simile to advocate that a virtuous ruler should govern with the gentle and accommodating qualities displayed by water. He should assist and provide for the people just as water does, rather than competing with them for resources. Later this term came to mean that one should act as water does in nourishing all things and do one's best to help others without seeking fame or profit. It also implies virtues such as endurance and modesty.

Addressing the welcome dinner of the 22nd APEC Economic Leaders' Meeting in Beijing in November 2014, Xi Jinping said: Over 2,000 years ago, Chinese philosopher Lao Zi noted that "The great virtue is like water, which benefits all of creation without trying to compete with them." True, water nourishes all things under heaven. We, APEC member economies, are brought together by the water of the Pacific Ocean. We have a shared responsibility to make the Pacific an ocean of peace, friendship and cooperation, an ocean that brings harmony, development, prosperity and progress to the Asia-Pacific region.

积善成德

“积善成德”出自《荀子》，意为善行好事，长期积小善为大德，就会形成一种高尚的品德。荀子认为，仅仅依循于人的本性，只能导致对外物无休止的争夺，并使群体陷入无秩序的混乱之中；而人的道德有赖于后天的教化，人需要在言行表现上符合礼法的要求，并经过长期积累，逐渐形成对道德、礼法的认同，确立起内在的道德意识。

2013年9月，习近平在会见第四届全国道德模范及提名奖获得者时强调，道德模范是社会道德建设的重要旗帜，要深入开展学习宣传道德模范活动，弘扬真善美，传播正能量，激励人民群众崇德向善、见贤思齐，鼓励全社会积善成德、明德惟馨，为实现中华民族伟大复兴的中国梦凝聚起强大的精神力量和有力的道德支撑。

Cultivating morality through good deeds

This term comes from *Xun Zi* (*The Book of Xun Zi*). It means that if one consistently performs good deeds, while the individual acts may be trivial, over time, one will cultivate lofty morality and achieve great virtue.

According to Xun Zi (c. 313-238 BC), also known as Xun Kuang, a thinker and educator of the Warring States Period (475-221 BC), if everyone follows their innate nature, there will be endless disputes that cause disorder and chaos among the people, while one's virtue can be cultivated through education from an early age. If one's words and deeds always comply with the norms of rites, gradually one will become a devoted follower of virtues and rites and develop an inner consciousness of virtue.

When meeting the fourth group of nominees and winners of national ethical model awards in September 2013, Xi Jinping said: Paragons of morality are important banners for building public ethics. We need to carry out campaigns to publicize such paragons of morality and let people learn from them, foster the true, the good and the beautiful, and spread positive energy. We should inspire the people to esteem virtue, perform good deeds and emulate virtuous people. Moreover, we should encourage the whole of society to cultivate morality by practicing virtue and to exert a positive influence through ethical behavior. In this way, we will marshal strong inner strength and ethical support for realizing the Chinese Dream of national rejuvenation.

自强不息

“自强不息”出自《周易》，意为自身努力向上，强大自己，永不懈怠。古人认为，天体出于自身的本性而运行，刚健有力，周而复始，一往无前从不停息。君子取法于“天”，也应该发挥自己的主动性、能动性，勤勉不懈、奋发进取，这是中国人参照天体运行状态梳理的自身理想。

中共十八大以来，习近平曾在多个场合多次提及“自强不息”。如2014年5月，习近平考察北京大学时强调，“天行健，君子以自强不息”；2017年12月，习近平在中国共产党与世界政党高层对话会上发表的主旨讲话中指出，中国人民没有向命运屈服，而是奋起抗争、自强不息，经过长期奋斗，而今走上了实现中华民族伟大复兴的康庄大道。

Making continuous efforts to strengthen oneself

This idiom first appeared in *Zhou Yi* (*The Book of Changes*). It means that one should make continuous efforts to improve and strengthen oneself. The ancient Chinese believed that the heavenly bodies follow their own nature and keep moving vigorously in an unending cycle. A man of virtue, who follows the law of heaven, should act on his own initiative and work diligently to strengthen himself. This is the Chinese view on self-development, based on the movement of the heavenly bodies.

Xi Jinping has on many occasions talked about the need for constant self-improvement. For instance, he emphasized on an inspecting visit to Peking University in May 2014, "As heaven changes through movement, a gentleman makes unremitting efforts to perfect himself." Addressing the CPC in Dialogue with World Political Parties High-level Meeting in December 2017, he said that the Chinese people have never yielded to fate; rather they have risen up and acted in a long-term struggle, so as to embark today on a broad road toward national rejuvenation.

无欲则刚

“无欲则刚”出自《论语》中孔子对弟子的评价：“子曰：‘吾未见刚者。’或对曰：‘申枨。’子曰：‘枨也欲，焉得刚?’”人的欲望太盛，便难有坚定刚强之德，难以刚正不阿、正道直行。“欲”指各种私欲、贪欲；“刚”即刚正公道、正直有力。“无欲则刚”是一种克己的功夫，讲的是立身处事尤其是执政做官的基本道理：一个人面对来自各方的种种诱惑，应该大公无私、端正品性、淡泊守志，不要有非分的贪图，这样就能一身正气，无所畏惧。

2018年3月，习近平在纪念周恩来同志诞辰120周年座谈会上指出，“海纳百川，有容乃大；壁立千仞，无欲则刚”。周恩来同志就是这样的人，他毕生严于律己、艰苦朴素，只求奉献、不思回报，并且告诫领导干部要过好思想关、政治关、社会关、亲属关、生活关，保持共产党人的政治操守和优良作风。

One is unyielding when one has no private desire.

This idiom is based on Confucius' observation on Shen Cheng, one of his 72 major disciples. As recorded in *Lun Yu* (*The Analects of Confucius*), the Master (Confucius) said, "I have never met anyone who is truly unyielding." Someone replied that Shen Cheng was such a person. But the Master said, "He is driven by desires. How can he be unyielding?" This indicates that if one has too many desires, one cannot remain firm, upright and honest.

The idiom is about the importance of restraining oneself. It is particularly true with the officials. They will remain upright and fearless if they can resist temptations and inducements, be selfless and indifferent to fame and fortune, and be free of irrational desires.

Addressing the meeting commemorating the 120th anniversary of the birth of Premier Zhou Enlai (1898-1976), held in March 2018, Xi Jinping quoted the Chinese saying, "The ocean is vast because it admits all rivers. The mountain peaks erect hundreds of feet high because they are free from any worldly bond." He hailed the former premier as an outstanding role model who was strict with himself, led a simple life, and made lifelong dedication with no expectation of recompense. The premier had exhorted the leading officials to stand the tests of their conviction, political integrity, attitude toward their social connections and relatives, and daily conduct, and observe the political norms and fine conduct of Chinese Communists.

浩然之气

“浩然之气”出自《孟子》，意为盛大而充盈于生命之中的正直之气，是一种宏大、刚强之气，是与道义相匹配的，由内而外，非得自于外。个人能够坚守善道，反省自身行事而无愧于心，“浩然之气”就会自然发生并逐渐充盈，使人勇往直前、刚强正直、无所畏惧。一旦形成“浩然之气”，就能摒除疑虑、果决勇敢。

2014年2月，习近平在俄罗斯索契接受俄罗斯电视台专访时表示，“读书已成了我的一种生活方式”，并列举出多项读书的好处，“读书可以让人保持思想活力，让人得到智慧启发，让人滋养浩然之气”。

Noble spirit

The "noble spirit," discussed in *The Book of Mencius*, refers to the mighty moral force that permeates the human body and enables one to be just and upright.

Such a spirit originates only inside the body and is not given by any external strength. If one can ensure good conduct, engage in self-reflection and have a clear conscience, a noble spirit will be nurtured and grow inside and make one courageous, strong and fearless. With such a noble spirit, no one will be hesitant, but will remain resolute and brave.

During an exclusive interview with a Russian television channel in February 2014, Xi Jinping said, "Reading is central to my life." He added, "Reading invigorates people's mind, gives them inspiration, and cultivates their noble spirit."

天下兴亡，匹夫有责

“天下兴亡，匹夫有责”流传极广。形成这一观念的思想渊源，可以追溯于《周易》《大学》《中庸》等典籍，以孟子之学最为集中。而“天下兴亡，匹夫有责”的说法则可溯源于顾炎武《日知录》，本意是指若整个社会出现道德沉沦，那么即使是普通民众也应当奋起救赎。1915年，梁启超有感于民国政府与日本签订不平等条约的屈辱，写下《痛定罪言》一文，认为欲雪国耻的关键在于“我辈之自新”：“斯乃真顾亭林所谓‘天下兴亡，匹夫有责’也。”

习近平多次引用“天下兴亡，匹夫有责”这句话。2014年9月，他在纪念中国人民抗日战争暨世界反法西斯战争胜利69周年座谈会上指出，在中国人民抗日战争的壮阔进程中，形成了伟大的抗战精神，中国人民向世界展示了“天下兴亡，匹夫有责”的爱国情怀。

Everyone has a duty toward his country.

This phrase is known to all in China. There are many similar expressions in such classics as *The Book of Changes*, *The Great Learning* and *Zhong Yong* (*The Doctrine of the Mean*). Mencius left the most citations about this idea.

The phrase finds its closest origination in *Ri Zhi Lu* (*Records of Daily Knowledge*) by Gu Yanwu (1613-1682), a thinker and historian in the late Ming (1368-1644) and the early Qing (1644-1911) dynasties. He meant that if the whole of society suffers a decline in morals, even an ordinary man must rise up to save the nation. In 1915, Liang Qichao (1873-1929), agonizing over the Republican government's signing of an unequal treaty with Japan, wrote an essay to call upon the nation to wipe out the humiliation through reform. He sighed in the essay, "Gu Yanwu was right to say that every man has a duty toward his country."

Xi Jinping has quoted Gu Yanwu on more than one occasion. At a gathering marking the 69th anniversary of the victory in the Chinese People's War of Resistance Against Japanese Aggression and World War II, held in September 2014, he said that the Chinese people had formed a great spirit of resistance during the war, as everyone showed their sense of duty toward their beloved homeland.

学者非必为仕，而仕者必为学

“学者非必为仕，而仕者必为学”，出自《荀子》，原文为“君子进则能益上之誉而损下之忧。不能而居之，诬也；无益而厚受之，窃也。学者非必为仕，而仕者必如学。”荀子和孔子一样，强调“学”是“仕”的前提和基础。为官从政不是为学的唯一目标，但是为官者却不能认为达到了目的就可以停止“为学”，反而要继续学习、提高修养，才能实现“齐家、治国、平天下”的理想。如果才学不胜而享厚俸，则无异于行骗盗窃。

习近平引用“学者非必为仕，而仕者必为学”，就是强调领导干部加强学习，不断提高工作水平和质量的重要性。2013年3月，他在中央党校建校80周年庆祝大会暨2013年春季学期开学典礼上引用这一古语，指出领导干部学习不学习不仅仅是自己的事情，本领大小也不仅仅是自己的事情，而是关乎党和国家事业发展的大事情。

One may not study with the goal of becoming an official, but officials must be learned to fulfill their duties.

This is a Confucian belief from *The Book of Xun Zi*. The original lines say, "If a man of virtue becomes an official, he will be able to gain fame for the ruler and alleviate worries of the populace. It is cheating if the incapable hold official posts; it is stealing if the incompetent receive high pay. One may not study with the goal of becoming an official, but officials must be learned to fulfill their duties."

Xun Zi and Confucius both emphasized that learning is the prerequisite and the base for starting a career as an official. To become an official should not be the sole aim of study, but one must not stop learning after becoming an official. Rather, one ought to continue with study and cultivation, in order to realize the goal of governance for all under heaven. It is no different from cheating and stealing if one is not capable or competent to serve in a post with high pay.

Xi Jinping has used this quotation and asked the leading officials to continue their study to improve their performance. At the celebration assembly of the 80th anniversary of the Central Party School and the opening of its 2013 spring semester, held in March 2013, he said: Whether the leading officials improve themselves through study is not a personal matter, but a big issue concerning the development of the Party and the country.

博学之，审问之，慎思之，明辨之，笃行之

“博学之，审问之，慎思之，明辨之，笃行之”，出自《中庸》。博学，就是广泛地学习；审问，就是仔细地询问，有针对性地提问请教；慎思，就是努力地、谨慎地思考；明辨，就是清楚地分辨；笃行，就是用学习得来的知识和形成的思想指导实践。这句话明确了从“学”到“行”这个过程里的五个阶段，也是循序递进的五个层次。

2013年3月，习近平在中央党校建校80周年庆祝大会暨2013年春季学期开学典礼上的讲话中引用“博学之，审问之，慎思之，明辨之，笃行之”，强调工作太忙绝不是放松学习的理由，学习要善于挤时间并且高效率地运用时间。

Studying extensively, questioning earnestly, thinking profoundly, discriminating clearly, and practicing assiduously

This is a quotation from *The Doctrine of the Mean*, indicating a correct approach to scholarly pursuit. One should first of all study extensively, then raise questions about a particular issue and think it over seriously, which may help discriminate between right and wrong. Then one needs to apply what one has learned in practice. These are the five progressive steps of the whole process from study to action.

Xi Jinping cited this quotation at the celebration assembly of the 80th anniversary of the Central Party School and the opening of its 2013 spring semester in March 2013. He said: Busy work schedules can never be an excuse for slackening the study, and the officials should be punctilious in making time for study.

学如弓弩，才如箭镞

“学如弓弩，才如箭镞”，出自清代诗论家袁枚的《续诗品·尚识》，大意是学识像弓弩，才能如箭头，学识决定才能，正如弓弩引导箭头射出，才会命中靶心。无论阅读别人的作品，还是自己从事创作，学识的高低与深浅，都会直接影响到欣赏水平或创作效果。因此，我们在日常学习中，也需要锤炼出扎实丰厚的学识，这样才能更好地利用自己的才干完成工作目标。

2013年5月，习近平在同各界优秀青年代表座谈时的讲话中指出，“青年的素质和本领直接影响着实现中国梦的进程。古人说：‘学如弓弩，才如箭镞。’说的是学问的根基就好比是弓弩，才能就好比是箭头，只要依靠厚实的见识来引导，就可以让才能更好地发挥作用。青年人正处于学习的黄金时期，应该把学习作为首要任务，作为一种责任、一种精神追求、一种生活方式，树立梦想从学习开始、事业靠本领成就的观念，让勤奋学习成为青春远航的动力，让增长本领成为青春搏击的能量。”

Learning is the bow, while competence is the arrow.

This quotation comes from *Xu Shi Pin* (*Sequel to Discourses on Poetry*) by Yuan Mei (1716-1798), a poet and critic of the Qing Dynasty. With this, Yuan meant that the foundation of learning is like a bow, while competence is like an arrow; only with rich knowledge can one give full play to one's competence and hit the target.

One needs to acquire extensive knowledge to better fulfill assignments, as knowledge will directly influence one's understanding of other's works and the quality of one's own works.

When speaking to outstanding young representatives from all walks of life in May 2013, Xi Jinping pointed out, "The qualities and competence of young people will have a direct influence on the course of realizing the Chinese Dream. There is an ancient Chinese saying, 'Learning is the bow, while competence is the arrow.' This means that the foundation of learning is like a bow, while competence is like an arrow; only with rich knowledge can one give full play to one's competence. Young people are in the prime time of learning. You should regard learning as a top priority, a responsibility, a moral support and a lifestyle. You should establish a conviction that dreams start from learning and career success depends on competence. You should make assiduous learning a driving force and competence building a resource for your youthful endeavors."

厚积薄发

厚积薄发，即充分地积累，少量地释放，多指学术研究或文艺创作等首先要广泛汲取前人已有的知识和成果，待有了深厚的积累和坚实的基础，再逐步从事学术研究或文艺创作，尝试提出独到见解或在前人的基础上有所创造。也指一个国家、一个企业在某一领域或某一方面经过长期的积累，开始逐渐展现其实力、创新力及开拓新的局面等。其核心内涵是，凡事不可急于求成，应注重积累，充分准备，才能把事情做好。

2014年10月，习近平在文艺工作座谈会上指出，古往今来，文艺巨制无不是厚积薄发的结晶，文艺魅力无不是内在充实的显现。

Accumulating enough knowledge for future application

This idiom means that one ought to acquire as much knowledge as possible for future application. It is particularly true with academic research or literary and artistic creation. Those who engage in such activities often have to first read and study extensively and draw upon the outcomes of their predecessors, so as to lay a solid foundation that will enable them to raise their own views or create their own works. It is also true with an enterprise or even a country: Only after long-term accumulation can they grow strong and be able to break new ground.

One should not be impatient for success. Rather, one should take time to expand knowledge and make preparations, which will pave the way for success.

At the Forum on Literature and Art, held in October 2014, Xi Jinping pointed out that masterpieces in China and the rest of the world, in ancient or modern times, are all outcome of long-term accumulation, and their appeal displays their inner strength.

温故而知新

“温故而知新”出自《论语》，意为温习旧有的知识，并获得新的理解与体会。前人对“温故而知新”的理解主要有两种：其一，将“温故”与“知新”理解为并列的两方面，认为在“温故”的同时就逐步获得新知，“知新”在“温故”的过程中得以实现；其二，将“温故”理解为“知新”的前提与基础，认为没有“温故”，就不可能“知新”，“新”是“故”的进一步发展，并且摒弃了其中陈腐的旧见。在今天，“温故而知新”已经超出一般学习方法的范畴，被视作个体、企业、组织甚至一个国家自我成长的基本机理，涵盖旧与新、古与今、已知与未知、继承与创新等辩证思想。

2014年9月，习近平在纪念孔子诞辰2565周年国际学术研讨会暨国际儒学联合会第五届会员大会开幕会上引用“温故而知新”，强调前人传承的知识积累了人们历史上对处理人、社会、自然三者关系的重要认知和经验，今人创造的知识形成了人们应对时代问题的智慧和探索，这两方面的知识对人类继往开来都十分重要。

Acquiring new ideas while reviewing old knowledge

Gaining new ideas and insights through reviewing old knowledge is a well-known idea from *The Analects of Confucius*.

Generally, people may understand this idiom from two angles. One, reviewing old knowledge and acquiring new ideas operate in parallel: One can gain new inspiration while reviewing old knowledge. Two, reviewing old knowledge is the prerequisite for acquiring new ideas: One who does not review old knowledge will not be able to acquire new ideas. In this process, the new will replace the old, and the outdated will be abandoned.

Today, this idiom is used in a wider context, not just as a method for individuals to learn. Enterprises, organizations and countries can all apply the idea in making constant progress. It is used to explain the dialectic relations between the old and the new, the past and the present, the known and the unknown, and the enduring and the innovative.

In September 2014, Xi Jinping attended the opening of the International Conference Commemorating the 2,565th Anniversary of Confucius' Birth and the Fifth Congress of the International Confucian Association. He used this quotation in his address and emphasized that the knowledge passed down from generation to generation is a summary of important perceptions and experience regarding the relationships between human beings, society and nature, and the knowledge created today reflects contemporary wisdom and exploration. These two kinds of knowledge are both important to human development.

读万卷书，行万里路

“读万卷书，行万里路”，出自董其昌《画禅室随笔》，意为要努力读书，尽可能多地了解书本知识，掌握间接经验；同时要尽可能多地接触实际，丰富自己的亲身体验，开阔眼界、增进见识。只有理论与实际相结合，间接经验与直接经验相结合，才能既有真才实学，又能学以致用。

2013年3月，习近平在俄罗斯中国旅游年开幕式上引用“读万卷书，行万里路”，指出中华民族自古就把旅游和读书结合在一起，旅游是传播文明、交流文化、增进友谊的桥梁，是人民生活水平提高的一个重要指标。

Reading 10,000 volumes of books and traveling 10,000 *li* of roads to become knowledgeable and experienced

This is an idea from a collection of essays by Dong Qichang (1555-1636), a painter and calligrapher of the Ming Dynasty. He encouraged people to acquire knowledge and indirect experience by reading extensively and to become aware of the true conditions in different places and broaden their horizons through personal experience by traveling to various places. A combination of theory and practice, direct and indirect experience, helps one become knowledgeable and capable and apply knowledge in practice.

At the opening ceremony of the Tourism Year of China in Russia, held in March 2013, Xi Jinping talked about reading extensively and traveling widely. He said: The Chinese people have a tradition of reading and traveling. Tourism is a bridge to disseminate culture, exchange ideas, and solidify friendship. It is a major indicator of improved standards of living.

千里之行，始于足下

“千里之行，始于足下”，语出《道德经》，意为哪怕千里远的行程，也要从迈第一步开始。这句话多用来形容大事都是由小事逐渐发展演变而来的，再远大的目标也要从点滴小事做起，逐步实现；引申说明任何事情都需要从头做起，一个好的开始往往是事情成败的关键，远大的理想和抱负需要脚踏实地地推动，才能完成既定的任务。

2021年11月，习近平在中非合作论坛第八届部长级会议开幕式上的主旨演讲中引用“千里之行，始于足下”，站在构建新时代中非命运共同体的历史起点上提出了4点务实主张。

A journey of a thousand miles begins with the first step.

This is a line from the *Classic of the Way and Virtue*. The philosopher Lao Zi indicated that major events often evolve from trivial things and great ambitions have to be achieved step by step. A good start is a job half-done, so to realize lofty ideals one must begin with the first step and get down to earnest work.

In his keynote speech at the opening of the Eighth Ministerial Conference of the Forum on China-Africa Cooperation in November 2021, Xi Jinping quoted, "A journey of a thousand miles begins with the first step," and made four pragmatic proposals from the historic starting point of building a China-Africa community with a shared future in the new era.

路漫漫其修远兮，吾将上下而求索

“路漫漫其修远兮，吾将上下而求索”，出自屈原《离骚》，大意为在追寻真理方面，前方的道路还很漫长，但我将百折不挠、不遗余力地去追求和探索。

2016年7月，习近平在庆祝中国共产党成立95周年大会上引用“路漫漫其修远兮，吾将上下而求索”，阐述从实现“两个一百年”奋斗目标，到实现中华民族伟大复兴的中国梦，中国正在奋斗的历史征程中，以此激励全党同志“不忘初心、继续前进”。

Long, long is my road, and far, far is the journey; high and low, up and down, I'll search with will.

This is a well-known line in *Li Sao* (*The Lament*), a poem written by Qu Yuan (c. 340-c. 278 BC) to express his determination to pursue the truth, not yielding to any setbacks, though the way ahead might be very long.

Speaking at the Conference Marking the 95th Anniversary of the Founding of the CPC, held in July 2016, Xi Jinping cited this quotation from Qu Yuan and encouraged the whole Party to stay true to their original aspiration and march forward on the journey toward the Two Centenary Goals and the rejuvenation of the Chinese nation.

穷则变，变则通，通则久

“穷则变，变则通，通则久”，出自《周易·系辞下》，意为事物达到极限就会发生变化，发生变化才能通顺，通顺则能长久，这是对事物变化规律的一种认识。也就是说，事物处于不断的变化之中，并会在极致时朝向对立面转化。人应该把握这一事物变化规律，在穷极之时寻找变化的契机，促成事物的改变，以实现通顺长久的发展。这一理念概括了自然变化的一个基本特征，即万事万物发展到一定阶段，会遇到瓶颈，原先有利的条件也会成为进一步发展的障碍。这时要主动适应，在变化中寻求新的发展路径，并通过不断动态调整，保证工作、事业能够稳定持续地发展。

习近平在纪念中国人民抗日战争暨世界反法西斯战争胜利69周年座谈会和在中国科学院第十九次院士大会、中国工程院第十四次院士大会上的讲话中均提到了“穷则变，变则通，通则久”。

Reaching the limit leads to changes; changes lead to solutions; solutions lead to development.

This is a saying from *The Book of Changes*, meaning that when all means to an extreme are exhausted, it will give rise to a desire for a change, while the change will lead to a solution and lasting stability. This is a keen perception of the dynamics underlying changes. In other words, all things are in a state of constant changes, and such changes will go into reverse when they reach the extremes. People should understand this and seize the right time and opportunity to bring about favorable changes and consequently realize smooth and lasting development.

This idea reveals a feature of natural changes, that is, all things may reach a bottleneck during the process of change, by which time previously favorable conditions will turn into obstacles hindering further progress. People should adapt to such situations, look for a new path, and make necessary adjustments in order to ensure smooth and steady progress.

Xi Jinping talked about the relationships between changes, solutions and lasting effects on a number of occasions, such as the gathering marking the 69th anniversary of the victory in the Chinese People's War of Resistance Against Japanese Aggression and World War II, the 19th General Assembly of the Chinese Academy of Sciences, and the 14th General Assembly of the Chinese Academy of Engineering.

君子一言，驷马难追

“君子一言，驷马难追”，出自《论语》，意为一句话说出了口，就是套上四匹马的快车也难追上。形容话已说出口，就没法再收回。也指代君子重诺，不会轻易违背自己的诺言，而中国人历来讲究以真诚之心，行信义之事。

2013年3月，习近平在接受金砖国家媒体联合采访时指出，中国已经多次向国际社会庄严承诺，将坚定不移走和平发展道路，永远不称霸，永远不搞扩张。君子一言，驷马难追，实践已经证明中国是说到做到的。中国也希望世界各国都走和平发展道路，共同致力于促进世界和平与发展。

A word once spoken cannot be retracted even by a team of four horses.

This is from *The Analects of Confucius*, meaning the same as the English idiom that "A word spoken is past recalling." What is said cannot be retracted, and this is particularly true with a man of virtue who values his promise and never easily breaks it. The Chinese people often use this old adage to make a promise with sincerity.

When answering a joint interview by the press of Brazil, Russia, India, China and South Africa, or the BRICS countries, in March 2013, Xi Jinping said: China has more than once stated to the international community that it is committed to the path of peaceful development and never seeks hegemony or engages in expansion. A word once spoken cannot be retracted even by a team of four horses. History shows that China has turned its words into actions, and China hopes that other countries will all follow peaceful development and contribute to world peace and development.

言必信，行必果

“言必信，行必果”，出自《论语》，意为说话一定要有诚信，做事一定要有成效。儒家认为，统治者要言而有信、取信于民，只有这样才能得到百姓拥戴，也只有这样百姓才能敢于说出真话。后世在运用这一术语时，多强调一个人应该讲求诚信、做事有始有终，不仅要兑现承诺，而且要言行一致。

2017年1月，习近平在中国共产党第十八届中央纪律检查委员会第七次全体会议上的讲话中强调，我们的先人们有大量劝导人们向上向善的警句名言，如“言必信，行必果”等，这些有益的思想观点，要结合时代条件加以继承和发扬，以坚守中国人的价值观，保持做人干事的精神风骨。

Being true in word and resolute in deed

This idiom originates in *The Analects of Confucius*. It advocates keeping one's promise and being resolute in one's actions. The Confucian school held that a ruler must keep his word and win the trust of the people, and only in this way can he win the support of the people and have the people tell the truth.

When we use this phrase today, we often emphasize integrity and the importance of honoring our promise and seeing it through.

At the Seventh Plenary Session of the 18th CPC Central Commission for Discipline Inspection in January 2017, Xi Jinping said that the Chinese ancestors had many sayings that encourage good faith and benevolent conduct, citing this one as an example. He pointed out that these helpful thoughts and ideas should be carried on under the current conditions, to preserve Chinese values and character in conduct and work.

吾日三省吾身

“吾日三省吾身”出自《论语》，意指每天多次反省自己、检视自己，发现自身缺点，弥补自身不足。“吾日三省吾身”是儒家所主张的一种道德方法，认为德行的确立取决于自身的努力和追求，因此需要时时反省自己的言行与内心，并以此作为修养道德的基本方法。

2013年6月，习近平在党的群众路线教育实践活动工作会议上谈及“照镜子、正衣冠、洗洗澡、治治病”的总要求时，指出正衣冠，主要是在照镜子的基础上，按照为民务实清廉的要求，勇于正视缺点和不足，严明党的纪律特别是政治纪律，敢于触及思想、正视矛盾和问题，从自己做起，从现在改起，端正行为，自觉把党性修养正一正、把党员义务理一理、把党纪国法紧一紧，保持共产党人良好形象。正衣冠往往一天一次不够，需要“吾日三省吾身”。

Examining oneself three times a day

This is a saying from *The Analects of Confucius*. It encourages people to repeatedly reflect on their own conduct every day in order to identify their shortcomings and fix their errors. This is an approach to moral examination advocated by the Confucian school, which believed that the effort one invests will determine one's moral attainment, so one ought to consistently review one's words, deeds and inner world in order to improve one's morality.

Speaking at the meeting, held by the CPC Central Committee in June 2013, to launch the Program of Mass Line Education and Practice, Xi Jinping talked about the general requirements to "examine oneself in the mirror, straighten one's clothes and hat, take a bath, and treat one's disease." He said: To "straighten one's clothes and hat" means that one should, after examining oneself in the mirror and based on the principles of serving the people, being down-to-earth in one's work and upholding integrity, dare to face one's weaknesses and shortcomings, strictly observe Party discipline, especially political discipline, start with themselves in facing up to problems, and take immediate steps to rectify their conduct. They should take the initiative to renew their faith in the Party character, review their obligations as Party members, and strengthen their resolve to observe Party discipline and state laws, so as to present a positive image as Communists. It is not enough to "straighten one's clothes and hat" only once, they need to "examine themselves three times a day."

从善如登，从恶如崩

“从善如登，从恶如崩”，出自《国语》，大意为顺从良善如登山一样艰难，屈从邪恶如山崩一般迅速。从善之难，从恶之易，是古代先贤的劝世箴言，广为后世政治家所重视。要舍恶从善，一是内心要有强大的信念做“防护堤”，二是要有良师益友互为提点。立志须坚，交友须慎，对于青年群体来说尤为切要。

2013年5月，习近平在同各界优秀青年代表座谈时强调，青年人要牢记“从善如登，从恶如崩”的道理，始终保持积极的人生态度、良好的道德品质、健康的生活情趣。

Virtue uplifts, while vice debases.

This is a quotation from *Guo Yu* (*The Discourses of the States*). It implies that following the good is as difficult as mountain climbing, while submitting to the evil happens as quickly as a landslide. This is an axiom authored by ancient sages and valued by statesmen of later ages.

To follow the good, one needs to have strong internal convictions as a moral core, and good external teachers and friends as guides. It is very important for young people to have firm faith and be selective in making friends.

When speaking to outstanding young representatives from all walks of life in May 2013, Xi Jinping said: Young people should bear in mind that "Virtue uplifts, while vice debases" and always be optimistic, behave with integrity, and lead a healthy lifestyle.

满招损，谦受益

“满招损，谦受益”，语出《尚书》，意为骄傲自满会招致损害，谦虚谨慎会得到益处。“满”即自满、自负；“谦”即“敬”，由衷地恭顺谨慎。古人认为，一切都在不断变化，优劣成败会转化；人需要与时俱进，不断努力，不能满足于已经取得的成绩而裹足不前；要谦虚谨慎、虚怀若谷，时时克服自身的不足。

2012年12月，习近平与在华工作的外国专家座谈时谈到“满招损，谦受益”，指出中国已经取得举世瞩目的发展成就，但仍是一个发展中国家，仍然面临一系列严峻挑战，还有许多需要面对和解决的问题。我们既不妄自菲薄，也不妄自尊大，更加注重学习吸收世界各国人民创造的优秀文明成果，同世界各国相互借鉴、取长补短。

Complacency spells loss, while modesty brings benefit.

This dictum is from *Shang Shu* (*The Book of History*). It means that one loses by complacency and gains by modesty. In the eyes of the ancient philosophers, all things are in a state of constant changes, and good and bad and success and failure are interchangeable. So one needs to keep pace with the times and constantly extend oneself, rather than being satisfied with progress already made; one should be modest and cautious and always review and overcome one's own shortcomings.

At a meeting in December 2012 with foreign professionals working in China, Xi Jinping warned that "Complacency spells loss, while modesty brings benefit." He said: Though China has achieved extraordinary successes, it is still a developing country and faces many real challenges and serious problems. It is neither unconfident nor over-confident, but will learn from the achievements of other countries and draw upon their strengths.

敬业乐群

“敬业乐群”语出《礼记》，意为认真恭谨地对待自己的分内之事，乐于与人相处。“业”本指学业，也可理解为自己所从事的职业、工作及分内之事；“群”本指同学、朋友，也可理解为团队和社会。“敬业”强调的是业务性，“乐群”强调的是社会性。具备这两方面特质，被认为是对每一个受教育者或职业人的基本要求，这也是构成健康、良好社会的基本条件。

2014年10月，习近平在文艺工作座谈会上指出，中华民族在长期实践中培育和形成了独特的思想理念和道德规范，有崇仁爱、重民本、守诚信、讲辩证、尚和合、求大同等思想，有自强不息、敬业乐群、扶正扬善、扶危济困、见义勇为、孝老爱亲等传统美德。中华优秀传统文化中很多思想理念和道德规范，不论过去还是现在，都有其永不褪色的价值。

Professionally dedicated and sociable

This idiom originates from *Li Ji* (*The Book of Rites*). It calls on people to be dedicated to their study and work and be friendly to their schoolmates, friends and other people. To be professionally dedicated and sociable is a basic quality of an educated person or an employee. These are also the basic building blocks of a healthy society.

At the Forum on Literature and Art, held in October 2014, Xi Jinping pointed out: The Chinese nation has fostered a unique philosophy and moral norms characterized by benevolence, people-orientation, honesty, dialectics, concordance and universal harmony. We have fine traditions such as seeking constant self-improvement, being professionally dedicated and sociable, fostering virtue and good conduct, rescuing those in danger, relieving those in need, and honoring filial piety to our parents and love of the family. These thoughts, ideas and norms all have indelible value today.

君子之交淡如水

“君子之交淡如水”出自《庄子》，意为君子之间的交情建立在道义基础之上，高雅纯净，清淡如水。君子之间的交往，与“小人之交”相对。“君子”是品德高尚的人，他们之间的交往是因为志同道合，看似平淡如水，实则情深义重；“小人”是品德低下的人，他们之间的交往是为了谋取私利，看似表面亲密，实则利尽义绝。“君子之交”自古为中国人所崇尚，其中蕴含着重道义、轻私利，褒君子、贬小人的价值观念。

2013年3月，习近平在参加十二届全国人大一次会议江苏代表团审议时强调，现在的社会，诱惑太多，围绕权力的陷阱太多。面对纷繁的物质利益，要做到君子之交淡如水，“官”“商”交往要有道，相敬如宾，而不要勾肩搭背、不分彼此，要划出公私分明的界限。

The friendship between men of virtue is as pure as water.

This is from *Zhuang Zi* (*The Book of Zhuang Zi*), a collection of the works by Zhuang Zi (c. 369-286 BC), also known as Zhuang Zhou, a writer and major Daoist philosopher of the Warring States Period. It means that men of virtue build their relationships on justice, and they only maintain ties with the people who cherish the same ideals. Such relationships are as pure as clear water and are based on deep affection and strong loyalty among those who cherish them. In contrast, shallow people often associate with one another for private gain, and their relationships look close but break apart quickly once the proceeds have been split.

Pure relationships of like-minded people have been treasured in China since ancient times, as the nation values friendship based on justice and disapproves of shallow relationships built on the pursuit of private gain.

When joining the deputies from Jiangsu Province to the First Session of the 12th National People's Congress (NPC) in March 2013, Xi Jinping said: Power is surrounded by too many temptations and snares. In dealing with material interests, the officials must treat the business people cordially, but not collude with them, and they must make a clear distinction between public and private interests.

民本篇

People-Centered Philosophy

民惟邦本

“民惟邦本”出自《尚书》，指民众是国家的根本或基础，只有百姓安居乐业、生活稳定，国家才能安定。“民惟邦本”的民本思想警示统治者要重视人民的力量，因而治理的关键在于实行仁政德治，以民生优先。中国共产党作为执政党，始终坚持“江山就是人民，人民就是江山”的鲜明立场，始终践行“全心全意为人民服务”的根本宗旨，始终依靠人民推动历史前进。

中共十八大以来，习近平在系列重要讲话中多次引用“民惟邦本，本固邦宁”的政治格言，充分表达了他一贯坚持的“以民为本，执政为民”的治国理念。2014年5月，习近平在北京大学师生座谈会上的讲话中将“民惟邦本”列为中华文化核心理念的第一条。

The people are the foundation of a state.

This idea comes from *The Book of History*. As the people are the foundation of a state, the state will have peace only when the people all lead a happy, stable life. This people-centered philosophy reminds the rulers to value the people, exercise benevolent governance, and take the people's wellbeing as the priority.

As the ruling party, the CPC believes that "The country is its people, and the people are the country," therefore it always serves the people whole-heartedly and relies on them to make progress.

Xi Jinping has on more than one occasion elaborated on the political dictum that "The people are the foundation of a state, and the state will have peace when the foundation is solid." This reflects his people-centered philosophy on governance and his commitment to exercising power for the people.

He cited "The people are the foundation of a state" as the first of the many quotations from ancient classics to share with the teachers and students at the seminar in Peking University in May 2014.

天时地利人和

“天时地利人和”出自《孟子》:“天时不如地利，地利不如人和。”此外，《孙膑兵法》也提到:“天时、地利、人和，三者不得，虽胜有殃。”这一观念强调作战时的自然气候条件、地理环境和人心向背等因素均应予以深思熟虑。“天时”本指作战时的有利气候，泛指时间上的各种有利条件，包括天气、时机、机遇等;“地利”本指作战时的有利地形，泛指空间上的各种有利条件，包括地形、地势、区位等;“人和”本指得到人们拥护，上下同心、团结一致，泛指人的优势。古人认为，它们是事关成败的三种最重要的因素，其中首要的是“人和”。这一观念反映了中国人考虑问题的三个基本向度——时间（时机）、空间（环境）和人，体现了“以人为本”的基本理念。

2013年6月，习近平在出席中墨企业家会议时指出，中墨经贸合作具有天时地利人和，发展前景广阔。希望两国各界携起手来，始终将对方发展视为自身发展的重要机遇，图发展、谋共赢，为中墨关系开创更加美好未来。

Good timing, geographical convenience, and harmonious human relations

The original expression in *The Book of Mencius* says, "Opportunity is important, even more so is geographical convenience, but most important of all is popular support." In *Sun Bin Bing Fa* (*The Art of War by Sun Bin*), the author, a military strategist of the Warring States Period, wrote that in the absence of any of these three essential factors, danger will lurk in a temporary victory. He meant that the outcome of a war hinges on the three factors: timing and climate conditions, advantageous terrain and location, and popular support and solidarity.

Traditionally these are regarded as the three essential factors of success or failure of any undertaking. They represent the Chinese people's emphasis on timing, space and human elements, with the greatest emphasis on human influence.

In June 2013, while attending a meeting of Sino-Mexican entrepreneurs, Xi Jinping pointed out that the prospects for bilateral cooperation were excellent, with a favorable domestic and international environment as well as popular support. He expressed the hope that the two countries would join forces, regard each other as sources of important opportunities for development and mutual benefit, and build a bright future for bilateral relations.

政得其民

“政得其民”出自《孟子》，意为治理国家要得到人民的认可，政令施行要重视民心民意。中国人认为，民心是最大的政治。一个政党，一个政权，其前途和命运最终取决于人心向背。

2014年10月，习近平在中共十八届中央政治局第十八次集体学习时的讲话中提到“政得其民”等古代治国理政经验作为当代国家治理的镜鉴，体现了中共中央以人民为中心的治国理政思想和密切联系群众的根本工作路线，展示了发展全过程人民民主、推进国家治理体系和治理能力现代化的中国智慧。

Governance must win the people's support.

This saying comes from *The Book of Mencius*. It means that the success of governance depends on the people's support, and the implementation of decrees must take the people's concerns into consideration. The Chinese nation believes that the people's support is of paramount political importance, on which hinge the future and destiny of a political party and a government.

At the 18th group study session of the Political Bureau of the 18th CPC Central Committee in October 2014, Xi Jinping referenced this saying and other ancient governance ideas as guides for contemporary practice. This showed the central leadership's people-centered approach to governance, how it values close ties with the people, and its effort to develop whole-process people's democracy and modernize the system and capacity for governance.

国泰民安

“国泰民安”出自《梦粱录》，意为国家太平无事，社会和谐安定，人民生活幸福。这是自古以来每一位正直的执政者所努力追求的治理目标和治理状态，也是每一个普通百姓所抱持的生活愿景。其关键在于“泰”与“安”，即安定、平和被认为是国家和人民的共同福祉，体现了中国人崇尚和平安定的精神。

习近平在发表2021年、2022年及2023年新年贺词时，都以“国泰民安”作为祝福结束语，表达了对开启新征程、开创新格局的美好希冀，也表达了对全国人民安居乐业的诚挚祝愿。可以说，这是他心系家国、情牵天下的生动写照。

The country enjoys prosperity, and the people live in peace.

This phrase comes from *Meng Liang Lu* (*Records of the Capital*) by Wu Zimu (dates unknown), a scholar of the Song Dynasty (960-1279). It depicted a state of peace in the country, harmony in society, and contentment among the people. This has been an ideal pursued by almost every ruler since ancient times. It is also an aspiration shared by the populace. Peace and stability benefit both the state and the people, and this again proves the value of the Chinese pursuit of peace.

In his New Year addresses for 2021, 2022 and 2023, Xi Jinping concluded his remarks with the same wish, "May our country enjoy prosperity and our people live in peace!" This is a sincere wish for the country on its journey ahead and reflects Xi's genuine concern for the interests of all the Chinese people.

政通人和

“政通人和”语出《岳阳楼记》，意为政事通达，人民和顺。“政通”即国家政策、法令等能够全面贯彻落实，政治事务运转顺畅有效；“人和”即人人各得其宜、上下一心、团结融洽。作为良好的治理状态，它与“国泰民安”相近，但更加强调“人”的因素，并凸显“政通”与“人和”互为因果的关系。

2017年3月，习近平参加十二届全国人大五次会议辽宁代表团审议时指出，一个地方要实现政通人和、安定有序，必须有良好政治生态。当代中国改革发展稳定任务之重、矛盾风险挑战之多、治国理政考验之大都前所未有，只有坚持全面从严治党，营造风清气正的良好政治生态，才能更好地凝心聚力，为干事创业激发内在动力、创造外部条件。

Good governance and harmonious society

This is an idiom coming from “Yue Yang Lou Ji” (“The Yueyang Tower”), an essay by Fan Zhongyan (989-1052), a statesman and literary scholar of the Song Dynasty. Under good governance, policies and decrees can all be implemented and political affairs run smoothly and efficiently; and in a harmonious society, the people are on good terms.

Such a state of governance is very close to the traditional ideal that “The country enjoys prosperity, and the people live in peace,” but lays more emphasis on the people factor and the interaction between a good government and a harmonious society.

When joining the deputies from Liaoning Province to the Fifth Session of the 12th NPC in March 2017, Xi Jinping said: To pursue good governance, harmony, stability and good order, there must be a healthy political environment.

At present, China has to undertake stern tasks in reform, development and stability, while encountering unprecedented problems, risks and challenges and facing the greatest test for governance. The Party must exercise strict self-governance and foster a healthy political environment so as to build cohesion and forge internal drive and external conditions for further achievements.

得道者多助，失道者寡助

“得道者多助，失道者寡助”，出自《孟子》，意为站在正义、仁义方面，会得到多数人的支持帮助；违背道义、仁义，必然陷于孤立。中国人自古推崇道义，认为道义是决定战争或事业成败的根本力量。只有奉行道义，才能赢得内部的团结一致、赢得民心，取得战争或事业的最后胜利；否则就会不得人心，陷入孤立无援的境地，并最终归于失败。

2015年9月，习近平在纪念中国人民抗日战争暨世界反法西斯战争胜利70周年招待会上引用“得道者多助，失道者寡助”，指出否认侵略历史，是对历史的嘲弄，是对人类良知的侮辱，必然失信于世界人民。

A just cause enjoys abundant support, while an unjust one finds little support.

This is from *The Book of Mencius*. The Chinese people have upheld justice since ancient times and believed that justice determines the fortunes of any war or undertaking. One who upholds justice will not stand alone, but will receive support, foster unity, and achieve ultimate victory, while injustice is doomed to isolation and failure.

At a reception commemorating the 70th anniversary of the victory in the Chinese People's War of Resistance Against Japanese Aggression and World War II, held in September 2015, Xi Jinping quoted this saying that "A just cause enjoys abundant support, while an unjust one finds little support." Attempting to negate the history of aggression is distorting history as well as insulting human intelligence, and anyone who attempts to do this will end up losing the support of the entire world.

得人者兴，失人者崩

“得人者兴，失人者崩”，出自《史记》，其含义有二：其一，民心、人心决定一个国家或政权的盛衰兴替。只有得到民心、顺应民心，才能保持国家或政权的兴盛不衰。其二，人才对国家、政权的兴盛与否起着至关重要的作用。也就是说，得到人心、获得人才就会兴旺，失掉人心、流失人才就会败亡；只有任人唯贤、知人善任，才能成就大业，保持国家和政权的长治久安。

2016年4月，习近平在网络安全和信息化工作座谈会上谈到，聚天下英才而用之，为网信事业发展提供有力人才支撑。他引用“得人者兴，失人者崩”，指出网络空间的竞争，归根结底是人才竞争。

He who wins the people wins; he who loses the people loses.

This is a phrase from *Shi Ji* (*Records of the Historian*) by Sima Qian (c. 145 or 135-? BC), a historian and writer of the Western Han Dynasty (206 BC-AD 25).

The phrase has two meanings: One, the people's support determines the rise and fall of a state and a government. Only by winning the people's support can a ruler ensure a lasting state and government. Two, talented and capable people are vital to the rise and fall of a state and a government. Only by winning the support of talented and capable people can a ruler ensure a thriving state and government.

Appointing officials on their merits and placing them in suitable posts according to their abilities can help maintain state power and ensure lasting stability.

At a seminar on cyber security and IT application in April 2016, Xi Jinping said: China needs to bring together the best minds across the world and draw on their expertise to develop its cyber security and IT application programs. "He who wins the people wins; he who loses the people loses," he cited this ancient saying and pointed out that competition in cyber space is in essence competition for talent.

不患寡而患不均，不患贫而患不安

“不患寡而患不均，不患贫而患不安”，出自《论语》，大意是对一个国家来说，不必去担心土地、财富、人口不多，而应该担心社会贫富不均，人民生活不安宁。如果财富平均，就无所谓贫穷和富裕，而人民团结一心，就不会觉得人口稀少，并且只有这样才能让国家和平安乐，不会有倾覆危险。这一理念是由中国传统文化中一直延续的奔小康、求大同的社会理想所决定的。中国人始终认为，一个美好的社会状态既然是由人民创造的，那么自然也应该由人民来共享。

2016年1月，习近平在省部级主要领导干部学习贯彻中共十八届五中全会精神专题研讨班上的讲话中引用“不患寡而患不均，不患贫而患不安”，指出共享理念实质就是坚持以人民为中心的发展思想，体现的是逐步实现共同富裕的要求。

What one should worry about is not the small population but instability, not poverty but uneven distribution.

This is from a dialogue in *The Analects of Confucius*. Confucius said: What the head of a state should concern himself with is not the lack of wealth or people but the lack of even distribution of wealth or the lack of stability. So long as wealth is evenly distributed among the people, nobody will complain about whether he is poor or rich; so long as there is solidarity, there will be no worry about the small population. This will bring about peace and contentment and protect against failure.

This belief is informed by the traditional Chinese pursuit of moderate prosperity and universal harmony. In Chinese philosophy, as a good society is created by all the people, it should be enjoyed by all the people.

At a study session on implementing the decisions of the Fifth Plenary Session of the 18th CPC Central Committee, opened in January 2016 for provincial and ministerial officials, Xi Jinping cited this quotation and said: In nature, the philosophy of shared development represents the idea of people-centered development, and it reflects the demand to achieve common prosperity in stages.

善治篇

Good Governance

天下为公

“天下为公”出自《礼记》，是一种美好的社会政治理想，意为天下是属于公众的，天下为天下人所共有，君王之位非一人所私有，而为公众所共有。这其中包含着反对世袭制，推举有才德之人的“尚贤”和“民本”思想，也蕴含着中国人所熟知的“大同”理想。“天下为公”为人们设定了理想而崇高的政治目标，描绘了远大而美好的社会愿景。

中共十八大以来，习近平多次谈及“天下为公”，彰显中国共产党胸怀天下的使命担当。2017年12月，他在中国共产党与世界政党高层对话会上指出，中华民族历来讲求“天下一家”，主张民胞物与、协和万邦、天下大同，憧憬“大道之行，天下为公”的美好世界。

All under heaven belong to the people.

This belief comes from *The Book of Rites*. It is an ideal of political governance. It means that everything under heaven, including the throne of the monarch, belongs to all the people. This implies an opposition to the hereditary system and an advocacy of recommending advancement based on virtue instead. It also embodies the people-centered thought and the ideal of universal harmony embraced by the Chinese nation. The state where all under heaven belong to the people is a lofty political ideal and a grand vision that has inspired the nation since ancient times.

Xi Jinping has more than once talked about this subject and the CPC's concern about the future of humanity. Speaking at the CPC in Dialogue with World Political Parties High-level Meeting in December 2017, he said: The Chinese nation believes that "All under heaven are one family" and that "All people are siblings, and all things are man's kin," and it values "coexistence of all nations in harmony" and "universal harmony under heaven." The Chinese long for an ideal world in which "When the Great Way rules, all under heaven are shared by all."

大道至简

“大道至简”是从《道德经》和《论语》的名句中凝练而成的，意为大道理（基本原理、方法和规律）是极其简单的，简单到一两句话就能说明白。“道”在中国哲学中，是一个重要的概念，“大道”即自然、社会的普遍法则以及人们对待自然、治理社会的根本原则；“简”即浅易、简明、便利。这一观念被广泛用于治国理政及社会管理等方面，主要有两层含义：其一，越普遍、越根本的道理就应该越简明浅易，便于人们掌握并付诸实施；其二，“大道”并不是远离人世间的高高在上的原理，相反，它的道理、功用就蕴含在人们的伦常日用之中，只要透过纷繁的表层现象，寻流讨源，就可以抓住事物的本质和规律，以简驭繁。

2017年1月，习近平在联合国日内瓦总部的演讲中引用“大道至简，实干为要”，指出构建人类命运共同体关键在行动，国际社会要从伙伴关系、安全格局、经济发展、文明交流、生态建设等方面作出努力。

Great truths are always simple.

This phrase is a summary of similar expressions from the *Classic of the Way and Virtue* and *The Analects of Confucius*. It means that great truths are often so simple that they can be explained in one or two sentences. In Chinese philosophy, *dao* (literally, the Way) is an important concept, and *da dao* (great Way, or great truth) refers to the general laws of nature and society and the basic principles that people follow in dealing with nature and in managing society.

The idea that "Great truths are always simple" has been applied in state governance and social management. It has two meanings: One, the more general and basic a principle is, the simpler and easier it is for people to understand and apply. Two, *da dao* is not isolated from the human world. Rather, it is embodied in daily affairs, and people can discern the essence of a matter and the relevant governing laws by looking through superficial phenomena and seeking root causes.

In his speech at the UN Office at Geneva in January 2017, Xi Jinping said: Great truths are always simple and they could be realized only through actions. Actions hold the key to building a community with a shared future for humanity. To achieve this goal, the international community should promote partnership, security, growth, inter-civilization exchanges, and the building of sound ecosystems.

天人合一

“天人合一”是一种认为天地人相通的世界观和思维方式。孟子认为，通过心得反思可以知性、知天，心、性和天之间是统一的；老子主张，“人法地，地法天，天法道，道法自然”。他们都强调人类社会与自然世界之间的协调统一关系，即天地和人之间的整体性和内在联系，突出了天对于人的根本意义，表现了人在与天的联系中寻求生命、秩序与价值基础的努力。“天人合一”理念作为中国“和”文化思想的重要组成部分，在中华优秀传统文化中具有独特的内涵与意义。

中共十八大以来，习近平多次谈及中华民族“天人合一”的崇高追求和生态智慧。2017年1月，习近平在联合国日内瓦总部的演讲中指出，人与自然共生共存，伤害自然最终将伤及人类。我们应该遵循天人合一、道法自然的理念，寻求永续发展之路。

Harmony between humanity and nature

This term represents a world outlook and a way of thinking which hold that heaven, earth and humanity are interconnected.

Mencius believed that through mental reflection, one could gain understanding of human nature and heaven, as mind, human nature and heaven are one. Lao Zi maintained that "Man patterns himself on the operation of earth; earth patterns itself on the operation of heaven; heaven patterns itself on the operation of the Way; the Way follows nature."

They both emphasized the unity between human society and the natural world: the integration and inherent relationship between heaven, earth and humanity, the fundamental significance of nature to humanity or human affairs, and the human endeavor to pursue life, order and values through interaction with nature.

The idea of unity of humanity and heaven is an important component of the Chinese culture on harmony and has unique significance in traditional Chinese culture.

Xi Jinping has more than once talked about the Chinese pursuit of harmony between humanity and nature and China's philosophy on the eco-environment. In his speech at the UN Office at Geneva in January 2017, he said: Humanity coexists with nature, which means that any harm to nature will eventually come back to haunt us. We must maintain harmony between humanity and nature and pursue sustainable development.

道法自然

“道法自然”出自《道德经》。“自然”指事物自主、自在的状态。“道”创造、生养万物，但“道”不会对万物发号施令，而是效法、顺应万物之“自然”。这揭示了整个宇宙的特性，囊括了天地间所有事物的根本属性，即宇宙天地间万事万物均效法或遵循“自然而然”的规律。“道”与万物的关系，在政治哲学中表现为执政者与百姓的关系，执政者应遵循“道”的要求，节制自己的权力，以无为的方式效法、顺应百姓的自然状态。道法自然、天人合一是中华文明内在的生存理念，是谋求人与自然和谐共生的中国智慧。

2020年9月，习近平在联合国生物多样性峰会上的讲话中指出，从道法自然、天人合一的中国传统智慧，到创新、协调、绿色、开放、共享的新发展理念，中国把生态文明建设放在突出地位，融入中国经济社会发展各方面和全过程，努力建设人与自然和谐共生的现代化。

The Way follows nature.

This idea first appeared in the *Classic of the Way and Virtue*. *Dao*, or the Way, creates and nurtures everything, yet it does not command anything, but follows and accommodates the natural conditions of all things. This is the Daoist interpretation of the common feature of the entire universe: All things between heaven and earth must follow and operate in accordance with their natural conditions.

In political philosophy, the relationship between the Way and natural things implies that between the ruler and the people. The ruler should follow the natural requirements of the Way, place limits on his power, and govern by means of non-interference to allow the people to take their own natural course.

Ideas such as "The Way follows nature" and "harmony between humanity and nature" are the underlying philosophy of the Chinese culture, which embody the Chinese wisdom to pursue coexistence of humanity with nature.

Speaking at the UN Summit on Biodiversity in September 2020, Xi Jinping said: From the traditional Chinese wisdom that the laws of nature govern all things and that man must seek harmony with nature, to the new development philosophy emphasizing innovative, coordinated, green and open development for all, China has always prioritized eco-environmental progress and embedded it in every dimension and phase of its economic and social development. The goal is to seek a kind of modernization that promotes harmonious coexistence of humanity with nature.

治大国如烹小鲜

“治大国若烹小鲜”出自《道德经》，意即“治理国家就像烹调美味的小菜一样”。这里以烹饪比喻治国，强调“烹小鲜”不能随意翻动，调料要恰到好处，火候要掌握得当，如同治理国家，必须要有审慎负责的态度。

2013年3月，习近平在接受金砖国家媒体联合采访时谈到，这样一个大国，这样多的人民，这么复杂的国情，领导者要深入了解人民所思所盼，要有“如履薄冰，如临深渊”的自觉，要有“治大国如烹小鲜”的态度，丝毫不敢懈怠，丝毫不敢马虎，必须夙夜在公、勤勉工作。

Governing a large state is like cooking a small fish: It must be handled with great care.

This adage comes from the *Classic of the Way and Virtue*. Just as cooking a small fish requires careful heat control, right seasoning, and a minimal amount of stirring, governing a large state is a delicate balancing act that must be performed with great care.

Responding to a joint interview by the press of the BRICS countries in March 2013, Xi Jinping said: In such a big, populous and complicated country as ours, we leaders must learn what the people think and what they want. We must act conscientiously and with the utmost care "as if we were treading on thin ice, or standing on the edge of an abyss." We must cultivate the attitude that "Governing a big country is as delicate as frying a small fish," never slacken our efforts or be negligent in our work, but always devote ourselves to work and the public interest.

为政以德

“为政以德”出自《论语》，意为以道德原则治理国家，强调道德对政治生活的决定作用，主张以道德教化作为治国的原则。“为政以德”与政得其民、礼法合治、德主刑辅等共同构成儒家德治论的主张，表明儒家治国的基本原则是德治，而非严刑峻法，应高度重视道德建设特别是为政者的道德建设。

2016年1月，习近平在第十八届中央纪律检查委员会第六次全体会议上的讲话中强调，中华民族历来都有珍惜名节、注重操守、干净为官的传统，历来都讲“为政以德”“守土有责”，领导干部要秉公用权、廉洁用权，做遵纪守法的模范，同时要坚持原则、敢抓敢管。

Governance by means of virtue

This term is from *The Analects of Confucius*. It implies the critical importance of virtue to political affairs, and advocates taking moral edification as the principle for governance. This idea and such views as "Governance must win the people's support," "governing by both rites and the law," and "virtue as the mainstay and punishment as the supplement" together constitute the Confucian advocacy of rule by virtue. It is obvious that the basic Confucian principle for governance is rule by virtue, but not by severe punishments and harsh laws, as the Confucian school highly values virtue, particular that of the rulers.

At the Sixth Plenary Session of the 18th CPC Central Commission for Discipline Inspection in January 2016, Xi Jinping said: It has been a tradition of the Chinese nation to honor one's reputation and uphold integrity and clean governance, and we have such sayings as "governance by means of virtue" and "responsibility for one's jurisdiction." Officials must exercise power in a just way and in favor of clean governance; they must be role models in abiding by Party discipline and state laws, and always adhere to their principles and fulfill their duties.

厚德载物

“厚德载物”出自《周易》，意为君子应以宽厚的德行承载天下万物或他人。这体现了古人对自身道德修养及人与自然、社会和谐一体的追求，并逐渐凝铸为中国人树立的治国理政和为人处世的理念和理想，成为中华民族精神的基本品格。

2018年12月，习近平在庆祝改革开放40周年大会上指出，自古以来，中华民族就以“天下大同”“协和万邦”的宽广胸怀，自信而又大度地开展同域外民族交往和文化交流。正是这种“天行健，君子以自强不息”“地势坤，君子以厚德载物”的变革和开放精神，使中华文明成为人类历史上唯一一个绵延5000多年至今未曾中断的灿烂文明。

Great virtue accommodates all things.

This term is from *The Book of Changes*. It means that a man of virtue should accommodate all things and fellow human beings with ample virtue. This reflects the ancient Chinese pursuit of moral cultivation and harmony between man, society and nature. It later became a philosophy and ideal on governance and human relations and part of the fundamental character of the Chinese nation.

Speaking at the meeting marking the 40th anniversary of the launch of reform and opening up, held in December 2018, Xi Jinping said: Since ancient times, the broad-minded Chinese nation has pursued "universal harmony under heaven" and "coexistence of all nations in harmony" and confidently and generously maintained contacts and conducted cultural exchanges with other nations. China has old sayings such as "As heaven changes through movement, a gentleman makes unremitting efforts to perfect himself" and "Just like earth, which is generous and peaceful, a man of virtue should accommodate all things with ample virtue." It is this pursuit of improvement and openness that has made the Chinese civilization the only one in the world to develop in an unbroken line from ancient to modern times.

文以载道

中唐时期古文运动的领袖韩愈等人提出“文以明道”的观点，认为文章主旨应合乎并发扬圣人的经典。宋代理学家周敦颐进一步发展为“文以载道”，提出文学像“车”，“道”即是车上运载的货物，文学是用以传播儒家之“道”的手段和工具。这一观念强调文学的社会功用，指明文学作品应该言之有物、有正确的思想内容。

2014年9月，习近平在纪念孔子诞辰2565周年国际学术研讨会暨国际儒学联合会第五届会员大会开幕会上指出，文以载道、文以化人，当代中国是历史中国的延续和发展，当代中国思想文化也是中国传统思想文化的传承和升华，要认识今天的中国、今天的中国人，就要深入了解中国的文化血脉，准确把握滋养中国人的文化土壤。

Literature is the vehicle of ideas.

In the mid-Tang Dynasty (618-907), Han Yu (768-824), a writer and philosopher, and some others, as leaders of the movement advocating the prose style popular in the pre-Qin (221-206 BC) times and during the Han Dynasty (206 BC-AD 220), proposed that the purpose of writings should conform to and promote the classics of the ancient sages.

Zhou Dunyi (1017-1073), a neo-Confucian philosopher of the Song Dynasty, expounded the principle of literature serving as a vehicle of ideas. He concluded that literature is like a vehicle while ideas are like goods loaded on it and that literature is a means and a vehicle to convey Confucian ideas. This theory emphasized the social role of literature and stressed that writers should know what they are writing about to ensure that their works convey correct ideas.

Addressing the opening of the International Conference Commemorating the 2,565th Anniversary of Confucius' Birth and the Fifth Congress of the International Confucian Association, held in September 2014, Xi Jinping pointed out: Literature is the vehicle of ideas, and it has the function of educating the people. Contemporary China is a continuation and development of historical China, and contemporary Chinese thought and culture represent the inheritance and upgrading of traditional Chinese thought and culture. To understand China and the Chinese people of today, one has to understand China's cultural roots and the cultural soil that has nurtured the Chinese nation.

礼法合治

“礼法合治”意为治理国家要将教化与法律相结合。在中国古代国家治理体系中，“礼”源于儒家，“法”出自法家。儒家的“礼”讲究“自我修养”的提升过程，法家的“法”则坚持“严刑峻法”才是出路。教化社会以儒家学说为主，因为要激扬人性善的一面，但治理社会却要以法家为主，法家主张“以法治国”，即把国家社会个人的一切活动和行为纳入法制的轨道，认为这是儒家理想化为社会现实的最主要的抓手。可以说，“礼法合治”是中国历朝历代鼎盛时期的政治准绳。

2014年10月，习近平在中共十八届中央政治局第十八次集体学习时的讲话中提到，“礼法合治”等治国理政经验能给人们重要启示，要治理好今天的中国，既需要对中国历史和传统文化有深入了解，也需要对中国古代治国理政的探索和智慧进行积极总结。

Governing by both rites and the law

This term means that in governing a country, the ruler needs to combine the edification by *li* (rites) and the rule by *fa* (law).

In the ancient governance system, rites originated from Confucianism and the law from Legalism. Confucianism extolled self-cultivation, while Legalism held that severe punishments and harsh laws would work better. Educating the people relied on Confucianism, which encouraged bringing the good elements in human nature into full play, while governing society needed Legalism, which preferred rule by law – to place all activities of the country, society and individuals under the law – and saw the law as the best tool to turn Confucian ideals into realities. It may be said that combining rites with the law was the governance norm practiced in the heyday of all dynasties in Chinese history.

At the 18th group study session of the Political Bureau of the 18th CPC Central Committee in October 2014, Xi Jinping said: Ancient ruling approaches such as "governing by both rites and the law" provide great inspiration. To govern China well, we need to understand history and traditional culture and summarize ancient governance practices and wisdom.

艰难困苦，玉汝于成

“艰难困苦，玉汝于成”，出自《西铭》，意为贫穷、低贱、忧伤、灾难等各种艰辛困苦的外部条件，往往可以像打磨玉石一样砥砺人的意志，使之终有所成。这种不畏艰险、自我磨砺、以苦为阶，最终实现奋斗目标的意志和信念，成为融入中国人血脉之中的民族品格。

中共十八大以来，习近平多次在不同场合引用“艰难困苦，玉汝于成”。2018年7月，习近平在金砖国家工商论坛上发表讲话时就引用了这句古语，阐发改革开放40年来，中国走过了不平凡的历程，成功开辟了中国特色社会主义道路。

Success comes only through hard work.

This term comes from “Xi Ming” (“Study Motto”), an essay by Zhang Zai (1020-1077), a neo-Confucian philosopher of the Song Dynasty. It means that harsh external conditions such as poverty, humble origins, misfortune and disasters can temper one’s will like grinding a piece of uncut jade until it becomes a marvelous artwork. It indicates the strong courage and conviction that allow one to brave any difficulty and achieve great success. This perseverance is part of the character of the Chinese nation.

Xi Jinping has quoted this saying on more than one occasion. Addressing the BRICS Business Forum in July 2018, he said: Success only comes through hard work. During the past 40 years, China has made its way of reform and opening up with strenuous efforts and blazed a path of building socialism with distinctive Chinese features.

功崇惟志，业广惟勤

“功崇惟志，业广惟勤”，出自《尚书》，大意是取得伟大的功绩，在于志向远大；完成伟大的事业，在于工作勤奋。不管是国家要实现振兴，还是个人要成就事业，都必须具备两个条件，一为立志，二为勤勉。立志是前提，勤勉为保障，无志不足以行远，无勤则难以成事。

2013年10月，习近平在印度尼西亚国会的演讲中引用“功崇惟志，业广惟勤”，指出中国有信心、有条件、有能力实现自己的奋斗目标，同时也清醒地认识到，中国仍是世界上最大的发展中国家，在前进道路上仍然面临不少困难和挑战，要使全体中国人民都过上美好生活，需要付出长期不懈的努力。他引用这句含义隽永的古语，恰如其分地表明了立志与实干相辅相成的关系。

One must have great ambition and make tireless efforts to achieve success.

This belief comes from *The Book of History*. Either a country or an individual must have great ambition and make tireless efforts to achieve success. Without high aims, one cannot travel far, and without effort, one cannot succeed.

In his speech at the Indonesian parliament in October 2013, Xi Jinping used this ancient quotation to indicate the complementary relation between great ambition and hard work. He said: China has the confidence, conditions and capability to realize its goals. It also understands clearly that as the largest developing country, it faces many difficulties and challenges on its road ahead. To bring a good life to all the Chinese people, it has to make long-term, sustained efforts.

苟日新，日日新，又日新

“苟日新，日日新，又日新”，出自儒家经典《大学》，意思是如果能每天除旧更新，就要天天除旧更新，不间断地保持更新。这一理念从动态的角度强调勤于省身和不断革新的重要性，即生活从不眷顾因循守旧、满足现状者，从不等待不思进取、坐享其成者，而是将更多的机遇留给善于和勇于创新的人们。

2014年6月，习近平在中国科学院第十七次院士大会、中国工程院第十二次院士大会上引用“苟日新，日日新，又日新”，指出中华民族是富有创新精神的民族，创新精神是中华民族最鲜明的禀赋。

If you can in one day improve yourself, do so from day to day. Yea, let there be daily improvement.

This axiom is recorded in the Confucian classic *The Great Learning*. It emphasizes self-review and constant innovation and encourages people to weed through the old to bring forth the new. Life never favors those who follow the beaten track and are satisfied with the *status quo*, and it never waits for those who muddle along or sit idle and enjoy the fruits of others' work. Instead, it provides more opportunities for those who have the ability and courage to innovate.

Xi Jinping cited this ancient saying at the 17th General Assembly of the Chinese Academy of Sciences and the 12th General Assembly of the Chinese Academy of Engineering in June 2014. He said: The Chinese nation values innovation, which is an essential part of our national character.

经世致用

“经世致用”一词由明清之际思想家王夫之、黄宗羲、顾炎武等提出，指学习、征引古人的文章和行事，应以治事、救世为急务。“经世”即治理国家和社会事务，“致用”即发挥实际效用。这一理念倡导学术研究要关注现实，通过解释古代典籍来阐发社会政治见解，解决社会实际问题，以增进国家治理能力，实现民生安定、社会改良。其强调知识的政治价值和知识分子的现实担当，体现了中国传统知识分子讲求效用、专注务实的思想特点。

2014年9月，习近平在纪念孔子诞辰2565周年国际学术研讨会暨国际儒学联合会第五届会员大会开幕式上指出，儒家思想和中国历史上存在的其他学说都坚持经世致用原则，注重发挥文以化人的教化功能，探索把对个人、社会的教化同对国家的治理结合起来，达到相辅相成、相互促进的目的。

Acquiring knowledge for managing state affairs

This idea was put forth by Wang Fuzhi (1619-1692), Huang Zongxi (1610-1695) and Gu Yanwu, all thinkers of the 17th century.

They held that scholarly studies should be geared to meeting current needs and be of practical value to state governance and social management. While interpreting ancient classics, scholars should expound their views on the social and political issues of their day to help solve practical problems, strengthen governance, improve the people's lives, and promote social reform. This view emphasizes the political value of knowledge and the social responsibilities of scholars and reflects the pragmatic character of traditional Chinese intellectuals.

In his speech at the opening of the International Conference Commemorating the 2,565th Anniversary of Confucius' Birth and the Fifth Congress of the International Confucian Association, Xi Jinping said: Confucianism and other schools of thought in ancient China all advocated that study should be of substantive practical value in educating the people, so that edification of individuals and society could be incorporated into state governance to achieve complementary effects.

他山之石，可以攻玉

“他山之石，可以攻玉”，语出《诗经》，意为别的山上的石头，可以用来琢磨玉器。比喻借用他人的批评、帮助来改正自己的过错，借他人或他国的情况、经验、方法等作为自己的借鉴和参考，可以更好地提升自我。这一理念充分体现了中国人开放包容、虚心学习的精神。

2017年12月，习近平在中国共产党与世界政党高层对话会上引用“他山之石，可以攻玉”，指出中国共产党历来强调树立世界眼光，积极学习借鉴世界各国人民创造的文明成果，并结合中国实际加以运用。

A stone taken from another mountain may serve as a tool to polish the local jade.

This is a line from *Shi Jing* (*The Book of Songs*). It implies that advice from others may help remedy one's own shortcomings. It also applies to a wider context. For instance, a country can improve itself by learning from the experience and methods of other countries. This shows the Chinese people's openness to learning from others.

Addressing the CPC in Dialogue with World Political Parties High-level Meeting in December 2017, Xi Jinping said: As a Chinese saying goes, "A stone taken from another mountain may serve as a tool to polish the local jade." Advice from others may help remedy one's own shortcomings. The CPC always stresses the need to develop a global perspective. We have learned from and drawn on the achievements of other cultures and applied them in the Chinese context.

言者无罪，闻者足戒

“言者无罪，闻者足戒”，出自《诗经》，意为提意见的人只要是善意的，即使提得不正确，也是无罪的；听取意见的人即使没有对方所提的缺点错误，也值得引以为戒。这一理念告诫执政者要想治理好国家，必须让人们畅所欲言，形成健康和谐的人际环境，同时充分了解人们的意愿和想法，以便从各种言论中汲取有价值的意见，这体现了言论自由的思想和包容精神。

2012年5月，习近平在中央党校2012年春季学期第二批入学学员开学典礼上强调，领导干部一定要本着“言者无罪，闻者足戒”的原则，欢迎和鼓励别人讲真话。

Blaming not the speaker, but heeding the warning

This is a line from *The Book of Songs*. It means that a kind speaker should not be blamed even if his opinion is not correct, while the listener should heed the warning even if he does not have the shortcomings or errors.

This saying also exhorts the rulers to allow the people to speak their minds freely and thus create sound and harmonious conditions for interpersonal relations. At the same time, the rulers should be broad-minded enough to heed all kinds of opinions and solicit insightful views. A saying from the oldest collection of Chinese poetry, it endorses inclusiveness and freedom of speech.

Speaking at the opening of a training program of the Central Party School in May 2012, Xi Jinping said that leading officials must follow this ancient principle and welcome and encourage others to tell the truth.

集思广益

“集思广益”出自《教与军师长史参军掾属》，意为集中众人的智慧，广泛吸收有益的意见。这一理念提醒决策者要广开言路，虚心听取各方意见，在综合考虑的基础上作出判断和决策，绝不能自以为是、独断专行。“集思广益”不仅是汇集智慧的过程，也是调动众人积极性、达成行动一致性的过程。

2019年9月，习近平在中央政协工作会议暨庆祝中国人民政治协商会议成立70周年大会上指出，发展社会主义协商民主，要把民主集中制的优势运用好，发扬“团结—批评—团结”的优良传统，广开言路，集思广益，促进不同思想观点的充分表达和深入交流。

Pooling collective wisdom

This is an idea of Zhuge Liang (181-234), a legendary prime minister and statesman of the Kingdom of Shu during the Three Kingdoms Period (220-280). It reminds the decision-makers to encourage free airing of views and solicit opinions extensively to help make right judgements and decisions, rather than acting arbitrarily on their own. Pooling collective wisdom is a process of encouraging the people's initiative to act in unison.

Speaking at the Central Conference on the Work of the Chinese People's Political Consultative Conference (CPPCC), held in September 2019 to also mark the CPPCC's 70th anniversary, Xi Jinping said: We should develop socialist consultative democracy, make good use of democratic centralism, carry forward the fine tradition of "unity-criticism-unity," pool collective wisdom, and promote full expression and in-depth exchange of different ideas and viewpoints.

前事不忘，后事之师

“前事不忘，后事之师”，出自《战国策》，意为过去的事情不能忘记，可以作为以后行事的借鉴。这一理念提醒人们要从历史中吸收经验教训，以此作为今后的参照或借鉴。中国注重修史，就是通过总结前代治国理政的成败得失来警示、启发当代和后世。

2020年9月，习近平在纪念中国人民抗日战争暨世界反法西斯战争胜利75周年座谈会上强调，“前事不忘，后事之师”，伟大抗战精神是中国人民弥足珍贵的精神财富，将永远激励中国人民克服一切艰难险阻、为实现中华民族伟大复兴而奋斗。

Past experience, if not forgotten, is a guide for the future.

This saying comes from *Zhan Guo Ce* (*The Strategies of the States*), a collection of stories of political strategists of the Warring States Period. The idea reminds people to draw lessons from history to guide future actions.

The ancient Chinese valued the lessons of history. The rulers often drew on the successes and failures of previous dynasties to guide their current and future governance.

Speaking at a gathering marking the 75th anniversary of the victory in the Chinese People's War of Resistance Against Japanese Aggression and World War II, held in September 2020, Xi Jinping said: History, if not forgotten, can serve as a guide for the future. The great spirit of resistance is an invaluable wealth of the Chinese people, which will continue to inspire the nation to overcome all kinds of hardships and dangers and strive for national rejuvenation.

居安思危

“居安思危”出自《左传》，意为处在安宁的环境中，要想到可能出现的危难。这是一种长远、积极的忧患意识，告诫人们要随时有应对意外事件的思想准备。“居安思危”不仅成为历代有为的执政者时时警醒自己的政治理念，也是民众积极进取的一种精神体现。

2018年4月，习近平在十九届中央国家安全委员会第一次会议上指出，前进的道路不可能一帆风顺，越是前景光明，越是要增强忧患意识，做到居安思危，全面认识和有力应对一些重大风险挑战，着力防范各类风险挑战内外联动、累积叠加，不断提高国家安全能力。

Being alert to dangers even in times of peace

This idiom first appeared in *Zuo Zhuan* (*Zuo's Commentary on the Spring and Autumn Annals*), a book believed to be written by the historian Zuoqiu Ming (dates unknown). It is a far-sighted vision that calls on people to be prepared for potential dangers. It urges the rulers to reflect on their political philosophy and encourages the people to maintain an enterprising spirit.

At the first meeting of the National Security Commission under the 19th CPC Central Committee, held in April 2018, Xi Jinping said: The road ahead will not be plain sailing. The brighter the prospects, the more we should increase our awareness of potential dangers, raise our vigilance, and fully understand and effectively address major risks and challenges. We must prevent internal and external risks and challenges from interacting, combining and accumulating, so as to constantly improve our national security.

见微知著

“见微知著”出自《韩非子》，意为发现细微苗头，就能知道事物的演变趋势或整体状态。“微”即隐微、不明，指事物尚处于不易被察觉的潜在状态；“著”即显著、明显，指事物的本质已经充分显现或事物的发展已处于充分展开的状态。这一理念指明做任何事情，都要深刻认识、精准把握事物演变的内在规律，既要着眼全局，又要关注细微处，提前防范可能出现的问题。

2021年3月，习近平在中央党校（国家行政学院）中青年干部培训班开班式上强调，要提升见微知著的能力，透过现象看本质，准确识变、科学应变、主动求变，洞察先机、趋利避害。

From a subtle clue, one can see what lies ahead.

This idiom originates in *Han Fei Zi* (*The Book of Han Fei Zi*), a collection of the works by Han Fei (c. 280-233 BC), a thinker and major representative of the Legalist school in the late Warring States Period.

It is about one's ability to perceive subtle omens and foresee developing trends and the overall situation. In doing anything, one needs to gain an in-depth and accurate understanding of the evolving trends by observing both the general picture and the minor details, so as to take appropriate measures.

Addressing a training program for young officials at the Central Party School (National Academy of Governance) in March 2021, Xi Jinping urged the officials to increase their ability to identify the general trend from subtle clues, grasp the essence through the appearance, accurately perceive the need for, effectively respond to and actively bring about changes, and spot opportunities before others to gain the initiative.

防微杜渐

“防微杜渐”出自《后汉书》，意思是把差错、问题等消灭在萌芽状态，引申为任何事物都有一个由隐及显、由小及大的过程，其间还可能引发其他的连锁反应，对于隐患、问题等，如果不做好提前防范，及时堵塞各种漏洞，就可能会付出成倍的代价，甚至会酿成全局性灾难。这一理念要求人们深刻认识并精准把握事物演变的内在规律。

2018年7月，习近平在全国组织工作会议上指出，要教育引导年轻干部强化自我修炼，正心明道，防微杜渐，做到有原则、有底线、有规矩。这深刻阐明了年轻干部强化自我修炼的重大意义和目标要求，为广大年轻干部在实践中成长成才提供了重要遵循。

Nipping problems in the bud

This idiom originates from *Hou Han Shu* (*The Book of Eastern Han*). Things often follow a course of growth from small to big or from invisible to apparent, and a sequence of events may occur during this process. If preventive measures are not taken to address hidden dangers and close all possible loopholes, serious losses and even disastrous consequences may occur. So people need to gain an in-depth and accurate understanding of the dynamics underlying changes.

Speaking at the CPC's National Conference on Organizational Work in July 2018, Xi Jinping demanded that young officials strengthen self-cultivation, shape good character, foster positive values, prevent small problems from growing into big ones, abide by principles and rules, and stay within the boundaries of Party discipline and state laws. This highlights the importance of self-cultivation to the career of young officials.

公生明，廉生威

“公生明，廉生威”，出自《官箴》，意为处事公正才能明察是非，做人廉洁才能树立威望，是明清两代一些正直廉洁的官吏用以自戒的座右铭。时至今日，这一理念仍然是执政者应当遵循的重要标准：官员当以身作则，廉洁自律，克己奉公。

2014年1月，习近平在中央政法工作会议上引用“公生明，廉生威”，强调政法机关要完成党和人民赋予的光荣使命，必须严格执法、公正司法，要坚守职业良知、执法为民，教育引导广大干警自觉用职业道德约束自己，做到对群众深恶痛绝的事零容忍、对群众急需急盼的事零懈怠，树立惩恶扬善、执法如山的浩然正气。

Justice breeds trust, and honesty fosters credibility.

This is a maxim that was followed by many upright and honest officials in the Ming and Qing dynasties. It remains an important guideline for the officials of today, reminding them to impose strict self-discipline and honestly and selflessly serve the public good.

Speaking at a central conference on judicial, procuratorial and public security work in January 2014, Xi Jinping said: To accomplish their noble mission entrusted by the Party and the people, the judicial, procuratorial and public security organs must enforce the law strictly and administer justice impartially. Justice breeds trust, and honesty fosters credibility. The officers should uphold their professional conscience and enforce the law for the good of the people. They should follow their professional code of conduct, never tolerate what the people detest, act quickly if the people so require, and strictly administer justice with awe-inspiring integrity.

靡不有初，鲜克有终

“靡不有初，鲜克有终”，出自《诗经》，是召穆公斥责昏庸无道的周厉王的一句话，意为凡事都有开始，但很少有人能够做到善终。这一理念告诫人们，为人做事要有始有终、善始善终。

2015年9月，习近平在纪念中国人民抗日战争暨世界反法西斯战争胜利70周年大会上引用“靡不有初，鲜克有终”，指明实现中华民族伟大复兴，需要一代又一代人为之努力。他强调，中华民族创造了具有5000多年历史的灿烂文明，也一定能够创造出更加灿烂的明天。

Everything has a beginning, but not everything ends well.

This is a line from *The Book of Songs*. It was originally a criticism of King Li (?-828 BC) of the Zhou Dynasty (1046-256 BC) by Duke Zhaomu (dates unknown). Everything has a beginning, but not everything ends well. This reminds people to begin well and end well.

Speaking at the commemoration of the 70th anniversary of the victory in the Chinese People's War of Resistance Against Japanese Aggression and World War II, held in September 2015, Xi Jinping said: As an ancient Chinese saying goes, "After making a good start, we should ensure that the cause comes to fruition." The rejuvenation of the Chinese nation requires the dedicated efforts of one generation after another. Having created a splendid civilization of over 5,000 years, the Chinese nation will certainly usher in an even brighter future.

交往篇

Relations with Other Nations

以和为贵

“以和为贵”出自《论语》，意为礼之运用，贵在能和，就是主张借礼法的作用来保持人与人之间的和谐关系。以和为贵，是儒家倡导的道德实践原则，表明中华民族历来爱好和平，“和”的民族基因从未变异，“和”的文化源远流长。和平、和睦、和谐的追求深深植根于中华民族的精神世界之中，融化在中华民族的血液里。

2017年1月，习近平在联合国日内瓦总部的演讲中强调，中华文明历来崇尚“以和为贵”。中国人民深信，只有和平安宁才能繁荣发展。中国从一个积贫积弱的国家发展成为世界第二大经济体，靠的不是对外军事扩张和殖民掠夺，而是人民勤劳、维护和平。中国将始终不渝走和平发展道路。

Harmony is invaluable.

This term comes from *The Analects of Confucius*. The original text says, "In conducting the rituals, the principle of harmony is the most valuable." Here, the rituals are used to help maintain harmonious relations among people. This reflects the Confucian advocacy of harmony and also shows the Chinese nation's love for peace.

Harmony has been part of the Chinese people's DNA since ancient times, and the culture of harmony has a long history. The pursuit of peace, amity and harmony is an integral part of the Chinese character that runs deep in the blood of the Chinese people.

In his speech at the UN Office at Geneva in January 2017, Xi Jinping said: Peace is cherished in the Chinese culture. We Chinese firmly believe that peace and stability are the only way to development and prosperity. China has grown from a poor and weak country to the second largest economy not through military expansion or colonial plunder, but through the hard work of its people and their efforts to uphold peace. China will never waver in its pursuit of peaceful development.

和而不同

“和而不同”出自《论语》，意指君子能够与他人和谐相处，却不盲从附和。“同”与“和”是对待社会群体的两种态度。“同”指对事物差异性的抹杀，“和”则意味着对事物差异性的认同。中华文化主张在尊重事物差异性和多样性的基础上，实现整体的和谐共存，认为不同的事物只有彼此间相互辅助、补充，才能组成一个充满生机、富于创造性的和谐整体。

习近平在2015年第七十届联合国大会一般性辩论时的讲话以及在2017年联合国日内瓦总部的演讲中，分别基于人类历史发展潮流大势，总结了中国自身发展的历史经验和文化传承，强调了“和而不同”的理念。“和而不同”理念作为中华优秀传统文化的一个重要标识，富有极其深刻的哲学思辨与中国智慧，体现了中华民族的价值追求与民族性格，是新时代推动构建人类命运共同体的重要思想基础与价值支撑。

Harmony without uniformity

This term is from *The Analects of Confucius*. A man of honor seeks harmony without monotony of views. Forging identity means setting aside the differences among things, while seeking harmony means recognizing such differences.

The Chinese culture advocates harmonious coexistence of the whole on the basis of respecting differences and diversity. Differences supplement each other to make up a harmonious whole full of vigor and creativity.

In his speeches at the General Debate of the 70th Session of the UN General Assembly at the UN headquarters in 2015 and the UN Office at Geneva in 2017, Xi Jinping analyzed the trends of human development, summarized China's experience and cultural history, and emphasized the concept of "harmony without uniformity." This is an important symbol of traditional Chinese culture. It embodies the profound philosophical thinking and wisdom and reflects the pursuit and character of the Chinese nation. It also provides theoretical and value support for building a community with a shared future for humanity in the new era.

求同存异

“求同存异”出自《礼记》，意为找出共同点，保留不同意见。辩证来看，一切事物的差异都是相对的，都存在相互转化的可能。儒家文化强调，在处理人与人、国家与国家的关系时，需要承认彼此间的差异，通过协调达到一种“和而不同”的状态。在当今的世界环境中，承认文化和价值的多元，不追求绝对的一致，努力寻求彼此的共同点，达成双方的最大共识，正是中国对外关系的核心理念。

习近平在多个场合提及“求同存异”理念。2022年1月，他在世界经济论坛演讲中指出，不同国家、不同文明要在彼此尊重中共同发展、在求同存异中合作共赢。他同时强调，我们要顺应历史大势，致力于稳定国际秩序，弘扬全人类共同价值，推动构建人类命运共同体。

Seeking common ground while setting aside differences

This idiom comes from *The Book of Rites*. Dialectically speaking, the differences in all things are relative and interchangeable. The Confucian culture held that in handling the relations among people and between states, one needs to recognize their differences and seek common ground while setting aside differences.

In today's world, we should acknowledge the differences among cultures and values and seek common ground instead of absolute uniformity, so as to reach the broadest possible consensus. This is the core value prevailing in China's foreign relations.

Xi Jinping has reiterated the importance of "seeking common ground" on more than one occasion. For instance, at the World Economic Forum in January 2022, he said: Different countries and civilizations may prosper together on the basis of respect for each other and seek common ground and win-win outcomes by setting aside differences. We should follow the trend of history, work for a stable international order, advocate common values of humanity, and build a community with a shared future for mankind.

和羹之美，在于合异

“和羹之美，在于合异”，出自《三国志》，意指羹汤之所以美味可口，在于把各种不同的调料合到了一起，比喻只有团结各方面的力量，才能把工作做好。这一理念强调尊重事物的多样性，致力于多样性的和谐共生，这既是当今中国主张的不同文明相处之道，也是中华优秀传统文化的精髓。

2017年1月，习近平在联合国日内瓦总部的演讲中引用“和羹之美，在于合异”，阐明人类文明多样性是世界的基本特征，也是人类进步的源泉。面对全球性挑战层出不穷的当今世界，治本之策是构建人类命运共同体。面对丰富多彩与复杂多样的人类文明，各国理应摒弃“傲慢与偏见”，相互尊重、平等相待，和而不同、美美与共。

Delicious soup is cooked by combining different ingredients.

This apt expression is from the ancient history book *San Guo Zhi* (*The Records of the Three Kingdoms*). It also means that one can work well by unifying all forces. Respecting diversity of things to seek harmonious coexistence represents an insightful summary of the essence of traditional Chinese culture. It is also a Chinese advocacy for coexistence of diverse civilizations in today's world.

At the UN Office at Geneva in January 2017, Xi Jinping said: Delicious soup is cooked by combining different ingredients. Diversity of human civilizations not only defines our world, but also drives human progress.

As humanity is in an era of numerous challenges, China's proposition is to build a community with a shared future. In a world with colorful cultures, countries should abandon "pride and prejudice," respect each other, treat each other with equality, seek harmony without uniformity, and appreciate the diversity of civilizations around the world.

美人之美，美美与共

“美人之美，美美与共”，语出中国社会学家费孝通先生的主题演讲《人的研究在中国——个人的经历》，他以“各美其美，美人之美，美美与共，天下大同”这十六字箴言阐明如何处理不同文化关系，即要尊重其他民族文化，实现世界文化共同繁荣。中华文化向来认为，在欣赏本民族创造的灿烂文明的同时，也应该去欣赏其他民族的文明，在互相欣赏的过程中促进不同文明达到一种和谐状态，实现理想中的大同美。

2019年5月，习近平在亚洲文明对话大会开幕式上指出，应坚持美人之美、美美与共。每一种文明都是美的结晶，都彰显着创造之美。各种文明本没有冲突，只是要有欣赏所有文明之美的眼睛。我们既要让本国文明充满勃勃生机，又要为他国文明发展创造条件，让世界文明百花园群芳竞艳。

One should value not only one's own culture, but also the cultures of others, and this will contribute to the flourishing of all cultures.

This is a well-known saying from Fei Xiaotong (1910-2005), a Chinese sociologist, anthropologist and social activist. In a keynote speech, he proposed an idea about handling the relations between different cultures: "One should value not only one's own culture, but also the cultures of others, and this will contribute to the flourishing of all cultures." Such respect for other nations and cultures would bring prosperity to all cultures in the world.

The Chinese culture holds that nations should appreciate their own brilliant cultures as well as those created by others, during which process, harmony will be achieved among different civilizations, and thus the beauty of all is preserved.

Addressing the opening of the Conference on Dialogue of Asian Civilizations in May 2019, Xi Jinping said: We need to appreciate the beauty of each civilization and the diversity of civilizations around the world. Each civilization is the crystallization of human creation, and each is beautiful in its own way. Civilizations don't have to clash with each other; what is needed are eyes to see the beauty in all civilizations. We should keep our own civilizations dynamic and create conditions for other civilizations to flourish. Together we can make the garden of world civilizations more colorful and vibrant.

天下大同

“天下大同”源自《礼记》，是对中国古代追求的理想世界的描述，代表着人类对未来社会的美好憧憬，即天下一家、人人平等、友爱互助。随着时代变迁，这一理念融入了全球范围的政治、经济、科技、文化融合等思想。尽管大同理想为中国原创，但西方的乌托邦、现代的共产主义、地球村等愿景也与之有着极大的相似之处。

习近平汲取中华优秀传统文化的思想精华，多次提及“天下大同”的观点。2018年12月，习近平在庆祝改革开放40周年大会上指出，自古以来，中华民族就以“天下大同”“协和万邦”的宽广胸怀，自信而又大度地开展同域外民族交往和文化交流，曾经谱写了万里驼铃万里波的浩浩丝路长歌，也曾经创造了万国衣冠会长安的盛唐气象。

Universal harmony under heaven

This is an ideal world described in *The Book of Rites*, a vision pursued by the ancient Chinese. In such a world, the people under heaven are of one family, and everyone is equal, friendly and ready to help each other. This is called *da tong* (universal harmony) in Chinese.

As time goes by, other ideas about politics, the economy, science and technology, and cultural assimilation have been incorporated into this aspiration.

The *da tong* ideal was created by China, but it has many similarities with the Western idea of utopia, and the modern visions of communism and a global village.

Xi Jinping has referred to the traditional ideal of "universal harmony" on several occasions. Speaking at the meeting marking the 40th anniversary of the launch of reform and opening up, held in December 2018, he said: Since ancient times, the broad-minded Chinese nation has pursued "universal harmony under heaven" and "coexistence of all nations in harmony," and confidently and generously maintained contacts and conducted cultural exchanges with other nations. The camel bells along the Silk Road and the numerous foreign visitors to Chang'an, the prosperous capital of the Tang Dynasty, were all memories of a good past.

国虽大，好战必亡

《司马法》之《仁本》篇写道：“国虽大，好战必亡；天下虽安，忘战必危”。这一箴言意指一个国家无论再怎么强大，如果不断进行战争也会灭亡；天下虽然安定但要居安思危，一味享乐、忘记备战就会出现危机。中国古人认为，应该本着仁爱精神处理问题，即便是正义战争，也会消耗国力。这种思想既体现了战争与国家兴衰的辩证关系，也彰显了中华民族爱好和平的精神。

习近平曾在多个外交场合引用“国虽大，好战必亡”。2014年5月，他在中国国际友好大会暨中国人民对外友好协会成立60周年纪念活动上指出，中国的先人早就知道“国虽大，好战必亡”的道理。中国坚持走和平发展道路，中国人民愿意同世界各国人民和睦相处、和谐发展，共谋和平、共护和平、共享和平。

A warlike state, however big it may be, will eventually perish.

In *Si Ma Fa* (*The Marshal's Art of War*), it was written, "A warlike state, however big it may be, will eventually perish; the world in peace, if relaxing vigilance against war, will face danger."

The ancient Chinese held that benevolence should be applied in handling disputes and that a war of justice would also exhaust a nation's resources. This idea reflects the dialectical relation between war and state power and proves the Chinese love for peace.

Xi Jinping has talked about this idea on several diplomatic occasions. At the China International Friendship Conference in Commemoration of the 60th Anniversary of the Chinese People's Association for Friendship with Foreign Countries, held in May 2014, he said: The Chinese ancestors knew that "A warlike state, however big it may be, will eventually perish." China will follow peaceful development, and the Chinese people are willing to coexist with other nations in harmony and peace and pursue, protect and enjoy peace together.

兼爱非攻

“兼爱非攻”是墨家的基本主张。“兼爱”强调每个人都应像爱自己一样爱他人，像爱自己的家人、国人一样爱别人的家人、爱别国的国人，那么人与人之间就会彼此相爱。这种相爱是不分亲疏远近、尊卑上下的，是平等的、没有差别的爱。只要做到“兼爱”，就能够避免人与人、家与家、国与国之间的相互攻伐、侵害，进而实现互利。“非攻”即反对不义的战争。墨家认为，违反道义的攻伐有着严重危害，不仅被攻伐的国家会遭到极大破坏，发动战争的国家也会面临大量的人员伤亡及财产损失，因此应该禁止不义的战争。

2014年6月，习近平在和平共处五项原则发表60周年纪念大会上指出，和平共处五项原则之所以在亚洲诞生，是因为它传承了亚洲人民崇尚和平的思想传统，中华民族历来崇尚“协和万邦”“兼爱非攻”等理念。

Universal love and non-aggression

These are two basic doctrines of the Mohist school of thought.

Universal love means that you should love others as you love yourself and love others' relatives and the people of other states as you love your own, so that all people will love one another. Such affection does not stem from blood ties or social status. It is equal, without differentiation. With universal love among all, conflict can be avoided between individuals, family clans and states, and all can enjoy equal benefit.

Non-aggression means opposition to unjust warfare. The Mohists regarded immoral aggressive wars as acutely harmful to society. Not only does the state being attacked suffer great damage, the state that starts the war also suffers serious casualties and property losses. Therefore, unjust wars should be averted.

At the meeting marking the 60th anniversary of the initiation of the Five Principles of Peaceful Coexistence, held in June 2014, Xi Jinping pointed out: It is no coincidence that the Five Principles of Peaceful Coexistence were born in Asia, because they embody the Asian tradition of loving peace. He said that the Chinese nation has always held such beliefs as "peace among all nations" and "universal love and non-aggression."

己所不欲，勿施于人

“己所不欲，勿施于人”，出自《论语》，意为自己不喜欢的，也不要强加给对方。这一箴言强调设身处地、换位思考，认为人应该以对待自身行为的态度为参照物来对待他人，要宽宏大量，宽恕待人。倘若把自己不喜欢的硬推给他人，不仅会破坏彼此关系，还会让事情变得僵持而不可收拾。这是儒家处理人与人关系的重要原则，体现了尊重、仁爱、平等和宽容的基本精神。

习近平于2013年6月在墨西哥参议院的演讲、2014年3月在德国科尔伯基金会的演讲、2017年1月在联合国日内瓦总部的演讲、2021年11月在中国—东盟建立对话关系30周年纪念峰会上的讲话等多个场合，均引用了“己所不欲，勿施于人”这一箴言，阐明中国坚持和平发展道路，永不称霸、永不扩张、永不谋求势力范围。

Do not do unto others what you would not have others do unto you.

This is a line in *The Analects of Confucius*. It advises one to show empathy toward others, put oneself in another's shoes, and be generous and tolerant. Anyone who imposes their will on others will see their relationships founder. This is an important Confucian principle for handling interpersonal relations. The core values are respect, benevolence, equality and tolerance.

Xi Jinping cited this quotation at the Mexican Senate in June 2013, the German Körber-Stiftung in March 2014, the UN Office at Geneva in January 2017, and the Special Summit to Commemorate the 30th Anniversary of the China-ASEAN Dialogue Relations in November 2021, thereby reiterating that China will never waver in its pursuit of peaceful development and never seek hegemony, expansion or spheres of influence.

恃德者昌，恃力者亡

“恃德者昌，恃力者亡”，语出《史记》，意为依靠美德行事的人一定兴旺发达，凭借暴力行事的人必将走向灭亡。中国人自古提倡以德服人，反对以权压人，认为只有用德行才能让人心悦诚服，而权力只能使人被迫屈从，不能达成真实持久的和谐团结。

2016年4月，习近平在亚洲相互协作与信任措施会议第五次外长会议开幕式上引用“恃德者昌，恃力者亡”一语，倡议树立共同、综合、合作、可持续的亚洲安全观，提出应依据国际法，坚持对话协商，以和平方式解决争议问题，并通过对话增互信、解纷争、促安全，共创亚洲和平与繁荣的美好未来。

He who cherishes virtue prospers; he who favors might perishes.

This is a warning from the *Records of the Historian*. It reflects the ancient Chinese advocacy of winning others' admiration with virtue and opposition to forcing others with power. Virtue can convince people and bring lasting harmony and genuine solidarity, while power only forces them to obey.

Addressing the opening of the Fifth Meeting of the Ministers of Foreign Affairs of the Conference on Interaction and Confidence-building Measures in Asia in April 2016, Xi Jinping quoted the Chinese adage, "He who cherishes virtue prospers; he who favors might perishes." He proposed a new Asian approach to common, comprehensive, cooperative and sustainable security and called for upholding peaceful settlement of disputes through dialogue and consultation in accordance with international law, and enhancing trust, resolving disagreements, and promoting security through dialogue, so as to bring enduring peace and common prosperity and open up a great future for Asia.

国不以利为利，以义为利也

“国不以利为利，以义为利也”，出自《大学》，意为治理国家不应以财富为利益出发点，而应以仁义为处事着眼点。“义”与“利”是中国人道德观里最基本的两个概念，一个是道德理性，一个是功利理性。在儒家看来，“义”与“利”都是人性的本能，人有逐利的冲动，也会有道德的萌动，只不过在价值判断上，不仅“义”要高于“利”，而且要用“义”来约束和引导“利”。

2014年7月，习近平在韩国国立首尔大学的演讲中引用“国不以利为利，以义为利也”，指明在国际关系中要妥善处理义和利的关系，践行正确义利观。

A state ruler seeks not wealth, but righteousness.

This line comes from *The Book of Rites*. Since ancient times, *yi* (righteousness) and *li* (gain) have been two basic concepts in the Chinese outlook on morality. One involves virtue and the greater good, and the other involves profit and material gain. The Confucian school of thought believed that profit seeking and moral pursuit are both instincts and natural desires. In terms of value judgement, people should favor the pursuit of *yi* over that of *li* and use *yi* to restrain and guide *li*.

At Seoul National University in July 2014, Xi Jinping said: As the ancient Chinese saying goes, "A state ruler seeks not wealth, but righteousness." We value the greater good and shared interests in international cooperation.

己欲立而立人，己欲达而达人

“己欲立而立人，己欲达而达人”，出自《论语》，意为自己要站稳，才能扶起摔倒的人；自己要腾达，才能博施济众。如果说“爱人”是“仁”的基本内涵，那么“己欲立而立人，己欲达而达人”就是“爱人”的行动指南。这包含三个层面的含义：第一，自己不想要的，不要强加给他人；第二，推己及人、设身处地地为他人着想；第三，在自己努力争取成功的时候，也要积极促进和帮助他人获得成功。

2015年4月，习近平在巴基斯坦议会的演讲中指出，中华文化倡导“己欲立而立人，己欲达而达人”，中国坚持正确义利观，帮助巴基斯坦就是帮助我们自己。

A humane person helps others establish what he himself wishes to establish and achieve what he himself wishes to achieve.

This is a well-known saying in *The Analects of Confucius*. He who can stand firm himself may raise those fallen; he who has succeeded is able to provide generous relief to the poor. To love others is the basic meaning of *ren* (benevolence), and to help others is how one loves others.

This saying has three extended implications: First, do not impose on others what you do not like; second, be empathetic and considerate; and third, help others do likewise while making your own effort for success.

Speaking at the Parliament of Pakistan in April 2015, Xi Jinping said: The Chinese culture believes that while achieving one's own success, one should help others achieve their success as well. China values friendship and shared interests. To help Pakistan is to help China itself.

穷则独善其身，达则兼善天下

“穷则独善其身，达则兼善天下”，出自《孟子》，意为不得志时就要洁身自好修养个人品德，得志时就要让全天下人都能得到帮助和利益。

2014年3月，习近平在中法建交50周年纪念大会上的讲话中指出，“穷则独善其身，达则兼善天下”是中华民族始终崇尚的品德和胸怀，中国一心一意办好自己的事情，既是对自己负责，也是为世界作贡献。随着自身不断发展，中国已经并将继续尽己所能，为世界和平与发展作出自己的贡献。

In difficult times, one focuses on self-cultivation; after achieving success, one brings prosperity to all under heaven.

This axiom comes from *The Book of Mencius*. It means that one should focus on self-cultivation and preserve one's integrity in difficult times and help others and bring prosperity to all under heaven after achieving success.

Speaking at the meeting commemorating the 50th anniversary of the Sino-French diplomatic relations, held in March 2014, Xi Jinping said: It has been the Chinese nation's virtue and character to focus on self-cultivation in difficult times and bring prosperity to all after achieving success. China has always been committed to managing its own affairs well. This shows how it takes responsibility for itself and makes contribution to the rest of the world. China has done and will continue to do its best to contribute to world peace and development.

亲仁善邻

“亲仁善邻”出自《左传》，意为与仁德亲近，与邻邦友好，是个人和国家都应该坚持的原则。这一理念强调“亲仁”是建立“善邻”关系的基础，即双方都应当共同遵循仁德，体现了原则性和务实性相统一的国际关系理念，展现了中华民族崇尚“仁”与“协和万邦”的基本精神。

2019年5月，习近平在亚洲文明对话大会开幕式上指出，亲仁善邻、协和万邦是中华文明一贯的处世之道。中国秉持亲诚惠容理念和与邻为善、以邻为伴的周边外交方针，深化同周边国家关系，打造周边命运共同体，充分体现了这一传统智慧。

Being benevolent and friendly toward neighboring states

This term comes from *Zuo's Commentary on the Spring and Autumn Annals*. It is a principle for handling the relations among individuals and between states. Benevolence is the basis for good neighborliness, and both sides should pursue benevolence. As applied to the relations with other states, it cherishes both principle and pragmatism and reflects the Chinese nation's pursuit of harmonious relations with other nations based on amity.

Speaking at the opening of the Conference on Dialogue of Asian Civilizations in May 2019, Xi Jinping said: For the Chinese civilization, pursuing amity, good neighborliness and harmony is the principle guiding our interactions with other countries.

China has followed the principles of friendship, good faith, mutual benefit and inclusiveness in its neighborhood diplomacy and forged friendships and partnerships with its neighbors to build a community with a shared future. This is a true reflection of the ancient philosophy of building friendship with neighbors.

投桃报李

“投桃报李”源自《诗经》，意为你赠给我木桃，我回赠给你木李，泛指互赠礼品、礼尚往来，即用礼物为载体，传达对对方的善意，表达与对方永结友好的诚意，隐喻平等互惠的关系原则。

2020年3月，习近平在同沙特国王萨勒曼通电话时表示，中国发生新冠肺炎疫情后，你第一时间向我表达慰问和支持，沙特政府和各界纷纷伸出援手，向中方提供了多批物资援助，中方铭记在心。中华民族是懂得感恩、投桃报李的民族。实际上，中国始终在力所能及范围内为国际社会抗疫提供支持，共同维护全球公共卫生安全，正是这一理念的有力印证。

Giving a plum in return for a peach

This idiom comes from *The Book of Songs*. It indicates an exchange of presents to express good faith and friendship. It also refers to equality and reciprocity.

In March 2020, Xi Jinping said on the phone with King Salman bin Abdulaziz Al Saud of Saudi Arabia: Following the coronavirus outbreak in China, you expressed sympathy and support to me at the first opportunity. Your government and your people have offered help and provided material supplies to China on more than one occasion. We will remember this. We Chinese people are a grateful nation and will repay your kindness.

On the part of China, it has done all it can to assist the international community in responding to the pandemic and protecting global public health. This is just another example of acting on the idea of "giving a plum in return for a peach."

志合者，不以山海为远

“志合者，不以山海为远”，出自《抱朴子》，意为如果两人志趣相同，他们不会因为有山海阻隔而感到彼此距离很远，交往的重点在于志向的相合、志趣的相投，阐发了志同道合的道理。

2013年3月，习近平在金砖国家领导人第五次会晤时的主旨讲话中引用“志合者，不以山海为远”，指出来自世界四大洲的五个国家，为了构筑伙伴关系、实现共同发展的宏伟目标走到了一起，为了推动国际关系民主化、推进人类和平与发展的崇高事业走到了一起。求和平、谋发展、促合作、图共赢，是金砖国家共同的愿望和责任。

Nothing, not even mountains and seas, can separate people with common goals and ideals.

This is a sentence in *Bao Pu Zi* (*The Master Who Embraces Simplicity*) by Ge Hong (c. 281-341), a minor official, medical scientist and Daoist of the Jin Dynasty (266-420). If two people have similar interests, they will not feel distant from each other though they are separated by high mountains and vast seas. What is more important is that they share the same aspirations and have the same inclinations.

In his keynote speech at the Fifth BRICS Leaders Meeting in March 2013, Xi Jinping said: As an old Chinese saying goes, "Nothing, not even mountains and seas, can separate people with common goals and ideals." The five countries from four continents are gathering here for the great goal of fostering partnership for common development and the noble cause of promoting democracy in international relations and advancing the peace and development of mankind. To pursue peace, development and mutually beneficial cooperation is our common aspiration and responsibility.

有朋自远方来，不亦乐乎

“有朋自远方来，不亦乐乎”是《论语》的开篇之语，意为那些志同道合的人，从各个方向、从各个地方聚到自己身旁，难道不是一件非常高兴的事吗？中国古人认为，要做成一件事，特别是要做成一件大事，必须要有志同道合的人。只有志趣相投的朋友在一起，做起事情来才是幸福的，做的事情才是有价值的。

2014年9月，习近平在参加纪念孔子诞辰2565周年国际学术研讨会时，引用“有朋自远方来，不亦乐乎”这句古语作为欢迎来自世界各国嘉宾及专家学者的开场白，表达了中国人民对朋友到来的愉悦，体现了中国人民广交天下朋友的胸怀与热情。

Is it not a real delight to have friends come to visit you from afar?

This is the opening line in *The Analects of Confucius*, expressing one's delight with like-minded people coming from different places. The ancient Chinese believed that to achieve great success one must have friends who cherish the same ideals and that working with kindred souls is a valuable, happy thing.

Xi Jinping began his remarks by saying "What a joy to have friends coming from afar!" to welcome the guests, scholars and experts attending the International Conference Commemorating the 2,565th Anniversary of Confucius' Birth, held in September 2014. This expressed the Chinese people's delight in greeting visitors from afar and also showed their hospitality to friends around the world.

四海之内皆兄弟

“四海之内皆兄弟”出自《论语》，意为全天下的人都亲如兄弟。“四海”即东海、西海、南海、北海，古人认为天圆地方，中国居陆地中间，陆地四周由四海环绕。“四海之内”指当时已知的人类生活空间，“四海之内皆兄弟”彰显了中国人兼济天下的博大胸怀、仁爱友善的人文精神。

2015年3月，习近平在博鳌亚洲论坛年会上指出，中国最需要和谐稳定的国内环境与和平安宁的国际环境，任何动荡和战争都不符合中国人民根本利益，中华民族历来爱好和平，自古就崇尚“四海之内皆兄弟”等思想。

All men within the four seas under heaven are brothers.

This is a quotation from *The Analects of Confucius*. The four seas refer to the seas on the four sides. The ancient Chinese thought that heaven was round and land was square, and China was located in the middle of the land, which was surrounded by four seas. The places within the four seas were all the territory known to them then.

The belief that "All men within the four seas under heaven are brothers" reveals the Chinese nation's concern for the whole world and kind offer of help to other people.

In his keynote speech at the Boao Forum for Asia Annual Conference 2015, Xi Jinping said: What China needs most is a harmonious and stable domestic environment and a peaceful and tranquil international environment. Turbulence or war runs against the fundamental interests of the Chinese people. The Chinese nation loves peace and has, since ancient times, held high such a philosophy that "All men within the four seas under heaven are brothers."

物之不齐，物之情也

“物之不齐，物之情也”，出自《孟子》，意为物品千差万别，这是客观情况和自然规律。这一理念强调事物的差异性，告诉人们不必把差别看作异类，而应将差异作为自己取长补短的补充。

习近平在论述国与国之间、不同文明之间的关系时，多次引用“物之不齐，物之情也”这句古语。2015年9月，习近平接受美国《华尔街日报》采访时引用这一古语，指出既然世界上存在着不同的民族、历史、文化、宗教、制度、发展水平、生活方式，那就肯定会存在一些相互之间不那么好理解的事情。但是，一切看上去不可理解的事情都是可以理解的，关键是要有去理解的意愿与行动，而不是彼此排斥、无法兼容。

Things are born to be different.

This is a line in *The Book of Mencius,* which states an objective law. The idea respects the differences among things and reminds people to regard differences not as aliens, but as a kind of supplement to offset one's shortcomings.

Xi Jinping uses this saying on many occasions to explain the relationships between countries and civilizations. In his written answers to the questions of *The Wall Street Journal* in September 2015, he quoted Mencius again and pointed out: With so much difference in ethnicity, history, culture, religion, social system, development level and lifestyle, there are things about others that one may find hard to understand. This is for sure, but that said, it is also true that anything that is seemingly incomprehensible can be understood provided that one is ready to learn and make an effort to understand it instead of dismissing it altogether.

独学而无友，则孤陋而寡闻

“独学而无友，则孤陋而寡闻”，出自《礼记》，意为独自学习而没有朋友一起切磋，就会知识狭隘、见识短浅，导致教育的失败；只有学习中相互观摩、取长补短，教育才能成功。事实上，朋友间切磋琢磨，也是中国传统儒学教育理论的一大特点，儒家始终认为互学互助是增长知识、修养德行的重要因素。

习近平在2014年9月纪念孔子诞辰2565周年国际学术研讨会暨国际儒学联合会第五届会员大会，以及接受美国《华尔街日报》采访等多个场合中，都引用“独学而无友，则孤陋而寡闻”来表达对文化交流和文明对话的态度。这一箴言提醒人们，面对人类社会创造的各种文明，既不能盲目自卑，失去民族自信力，又不能过度自傲，存有门户之见：一方面，各国要尊重自己的民族文化，另一方面，各国文明又要互学互鉴，共同推进人类文明交流交融，切不可自我封闭，更不能唯我独尊。

Learning alone without exchanges with others will lead to ignorance.

This is a warning in *The Book of Rites*. Those who study on their own and have no others to exchange views with may become narrow-minded and short-sighted and fail to make progress. Only through mutual learning and drawing on the strengths of others can a successful education be ensured.

Exchanging views is an idea championed by traditional Confucian philosophy on education, as mutual learning and mutual assistance are believed to be an excellent way to acquire knowledge and cultivate virtue.

Xi Jinping cited this idea in his speech at the opening of the International Conference Commemorating the 2,565th Anniversary of Confucius' Birth and the Fifth Congress of the International Confucian Association in September 2014 and in an interview with *The Wall Street Journal*. He expressed his support for exchanges among cultures and dialogues between civilizations.

Countries should neither feel inferior and lose national confidence in front of other civilizations in the world, nor be arrogant and parochial. They should respect their own cultures and learn from others to promote exchanges and interactions. They must not shut their door to the outside, still less indulge in self-aggrandizement.

万物并育而不相害，道并行而不相悖

“万物并育而不相害，道并行而不相悖”，出自《中庸》，这一理念阐明了中国人认识世界的基本方式，那就是万物竞相生长，彼此之间并不妨害；日月运行、四时更替各有各的规律，相互之间并不冲突。

2017年12月，习近平在中国共产党与世界政党高层对话会上引用“万物并育而不相害，道并行而不相悖”，指出文明的繁盛、人类的进步，离不开求同存异、开放包容，离不开文明交流、互学互鉴。不同文明应该和谐共生、相得益彰，共同为人类发展提供精神力量。

All living things may grow side by side without harming one another, and different roads may run in parallel without interfering with one another.

This idea comes from *The Doctrine of the Mean*. It explains how the Chinese people get to know the world, that is, all things grow together but do not harm each other, and the sun, the moon and the seasons rotate according to their own laws but do not create conflict among themselves.

Xi Jinping cited this quotation in his keynote speech at the CPC in Dialogue with World Political Parties High-level Meeting, held in December 2017. He said: The flourishing of civilizations and the progress of humanity will not be possible without enhancing common ground, openness, inclusiveness, exchanges and mutual learning among civilizations, and agreeing to disagree, and different civilizations should coexist in harmony with each other and draw on each other's strengths to inspire and nourish human development.

互学互鉴

互学互鉴是指在尊重文明多样性、道路多样化和发展水平不平衡等差异的基础上相互学习、相互借鉴，取长补短、共同提高。交流互鉴是文明发展的本质要求，文明交流互鉴应该是对等的、平等的，多元的、多向的，而不应该是强制的、强迫的，单一的、单向的。各国应该以宽广的胸怀打破文化交往的壁垒，以兼收并蓄的态度汲取其他文明的养分，促进文明在交流互鉴中共同前进。

2019年4月，习近平在第二届“一带一路”国际合作高峰论坛开幕式上的主旨演讲中强调了加强文明互学互鉴的重要性。他指出，我们要积极架设不同文明互学互鉴的桥梁，深入开展教育、科学、文化、体育、旅游、卫生、考古等各领域人文合作，加强议会、政党、民间组织往来，密切妇女、青年、残疾人等群体交流，形成多元互动的人文交流格局。

Mutual learning among civilizations

Mutual learning among civilizations means that different civilizations, following different paths and at different development levels, learn from each other and draw on the strengths of each other, to achieve common improvement.

Exchanges and mutual learning sustain civilizations, and such exchanges and mutual learning should be reciprocal, equal-footed, diversified and multidimensional; they should not be coercive, imposed, one-dimensional or one-way. Countries must be broad-minded and strive to remove all barriers to cultural exchanges, and they must be inclusive and always seek nourishment from other civilizations to promote common development of civilizations through exchanges and mutual learning.

In his keynote speech at the opening of the Second Belt and Road Forum for International Cooperation, held in April 2019, Xi Jinping reiterated the importance of mutual learning among civilizations. He said: We need to build bridges for exchanges and mutual learning among cultures, expand cooperation in education, science, culture, sports, tourism, health and archeology, and increase contacts between parliaments, political parties and NGOs, and communications between women, young people and people with disabilities, in order to facilitate multifaceted people-to-people exchanges.

海纳百川，有容乃大

“海纳百川，有容乃大”出自民族英雄林则徐的一副自勉联，意为要拥有像大海能容纳无数江河水一样宽广辽阔的胸襟和大气包容的品性。这一理念是在承认并尊重个体及社会差异基础上协调自我与他人关系、寻求社会和谐的一种道德自觉，但又不是故意纵容或作无原则的妥协。其提醒人们立身行事尤其是为官理政，要心胸开阔，善于听取各种意见，宽和对待不同事物，就像大海接纳无数江河细流一样，唯有如此才能养成伟大的品格，成就伟大的事业。

2017年1月，习近平在联合国日内瓦总部的演讲中引用“海纳百川，有容乃大”，强调国际社会要推进国际关系民主化，不能搞“一国独霸”或“几方共治”。世界命运应该由各国共同掌握，国际规则应该由各国共同书写，全球事务应该由各国共同治理，发展成果应该由各国共同分享。

The ocean is vast because it admits all rivers.

This maxim is a motto of Lin Zexu (1785-1850), an official of the Qing Dynasty well-known for his efforts to ban imported opium. It encourages people to be open-minded, generous and tolerant, just like the vast ocean that admits all rivers.

It reflects the moral sense of adjusting relations between oneself and other people to achieve social harmony, while recognizing and respecting individual and social differences. But it is not simply tolerance or compromise without principle. It reminds people, officials in particular, to be open to diverse opinions and treat all things kindly, like an ocean that embraces big rivers and small streams. This will help one shape a generous character and achieve great success.

In his speech at the UN Office at Geneva in January 2017, Xi Jinping said: The ocean is vast because it admits all rivers. He emphasized that the international community should advance democracy in international relations and reject dominance by just one or several countries. All countries should jointly shape the future of the world, write international rules, manage global affairs, and ensure that development outcomes are shared by all.

一花独放不是春，百花齐放春满园

“一花独放不是春，百花齐放春满园”，出自《古今贤文》，意为只有一枝花朵开放，不能算是春天来临，而到了百花齐放的时候，才是真正的春色满园。引申为如果世界上只有一种花朵，那么就算这种花朵再美，也是单调的。

习近平在论述文明交流互鉴和全球共同发展时，多次引用“一花独放不是春，百花齐放春满园”。2018年11月，习近平在第一届中国国际进口博览会开幕式上的主旨演讲中引用这一古语，指出在经济全球化深入发展的今天，弱肉强食、赢者通吃是一条越走越窄的死胡同，包容普惠、互利共赢才是越走越宽的人间正道。事实上，新时代的中国秉持平等、互鉴、对话、包容的文明观和共商共建共享的全球治理观，以更加开放的姿态拥抱世界，以更有活力的文明成就贡献世界，就是对这一理念的弘扬和践行。

A single flower does not make spring, while one hundred flowers in full blossom bring spring to a garden.

This is a saying collected in *Gu Jin Xian Wen* (*Proverbs Ancient and Contemporary*): The garden would be too dull if there were only a single flower, however beautiful.

Xi Jinping has used this old, popular saying to describe exchanges and mutual learning between civilizations and common development around the world. He quoted it again in his keynote speech at the opening of the First China International Import Expo in November 2018. He said: In a world of deepening economic globalization, practices of the law of the jungle and winner-takes-all only represent a dead end. Inclusive growth for all is surely the right way forward.

In the new era, China champions equality, mutual learning, dialogue and inclusiveness between civilizations, follows the principle of achieving shared growth through consultation and collaboration in global governance, opens its arms wider to embrace the world, and contributes the dynamic achievements of the Chinese civilization to a better world. This is a good example of how it puts this centuries-old belief into practice.

图书在版编目（CIP）数据

中国关键词．文明理念篇：汉英对照 / 中国外文出版发行事业局，当代中国与世界研究院，中国翻译研究院著；韩清月译．-- 北京：新世界出版社，2023.3
ISBN 978-7-5104-7535-1

Ⅰ．①中… Ⅱ．①中… ②当… ③中… ④韩… Ⅲ．①中国特色社会主义－社会主义建设模式－研究－汉、英 ②中华文化－研究－汉、英 Ⅳ．① D616 ② K203

中国版本图书馆 CIP 数据核字 (2022) 第 167750 号

中国关键词：文明理念篇（汉英对照）

作　　者：中国外文出版发行事业局　当代中国与世界研究院
　　　　　中国翻译研究院
翻　　译：韩清月
审　　定：徐明强
核　　校：张　彤
改　　稿：David Ferguson［英］
项目统筹：申　阳
项目执行：华光灿
责任编辑：楼淑敏　赵如意
责任校对：宣　慧　张杰楠
责任印制：王宝根
出　　版：新世界出版社
网　　址：http://www.nwp.com.cn
社　　址：北京西城区百万庄大街 24 号（100037）
发 行 部：(010)6899 5968（电话）(010)6899 0635（电话）
总 编 室：(010)6899 5424（电话）(010)6832 6679（传真）
版 权 部：+8610 6899 6306（电话）nwpcd@sina.com（电邮）
印　　刷：天津中印联印务有限公司
经　　销：新华书店
开　　本：880mm × 1230mm　1/32　　尺　　寸：120mm × 200mm
字　　数：120 千字　　印　　张：5.875
版　　次：2023 年 3 月第 1 版　2023 年 3 月第 1 次印刷
书　　号：ISBN 978-7-5104-7535-1
定　　价：68.00 元